THE WORLD WAR II
TOMMY

BRITISH ARMY UNIFORMS
EUROPEAN THEATRE 1939-45
IN COLOUR PHOTOGRAPHS

THE WORLD WAR II
TOMMY
BRITISH ARMY UNIFORMS
EUROPEAN THEATRE 1939-45
IN COLOUR PHOTOGRAPHS

MARTIN BRAYLEY & RICHARD INGRAM

The Crowood Press

First published in 1998 by
The Crowood Press Ltd
Ramsbury, Marlborough
Wiltshire SN8 2HR

enquiries@crowood.com

www.crowood.com

Paperback edition 2007

This impression 2020

British Library Cataloguing-in-Publication Data
A catalogue record for this book is available from the British
Library.

ISBN 978 1 86126 914 0

Edited by Martin Windrow
Designed by Frank Ainscough / Compendium

Printed and bound by Times Offset, Malaysia.

Dedication
To our sons Toby and James
that your dreams may become ambitions,
your ambitions realty.

Related titles by the same authors

Khaki Drill & Jungle Green
Martin J. Brtayley and Richard Ingram

**Europa Militaria 32: British Web
Equipment of the First and Second World Wars**
Martin J. Brayley

Contents

While the arrangement of this book is basically chronological, and we have been to some pains to avoid inconsistent combinations of kit within any one photograph, this index cannot be as consistent. Some items of uniform and equipment were on issue throughout the war years, others were introduced or developed progressively. Since some items inevitably appear in many photographs, this listing should be read only as a guide to the main subjects in each section, or to their first appearance. Certain items are listed more than once, to draw the reader's attention to useful photographs in later sections.

Foreword

Over the twenty - five years or so since I first became involved in military publishing I have found great interest and pleasure in widely different subjects; but during the last decade I have gradually become aware of both a lack and an opportunity, which seemed to me to be converging. This book is the point at which they have met, and it gives me great pleasure to have played a small part in making that meeting possible. The lack has been the absence of a particular sort of published treatment of the British soldier of World War II - a study of exactly what he looked like, and why. The opportunity has been the steady maturing of the technique of colour photographic recreation of historical subjects, pioneered by François Vauvillier and his colleagues in France.

The relative poverty of British World War II reference sources for the serious researcher and collector when compared with the continuing flood of German material was perhaps understandable in earlier years. In the eyes of the collector the foreign is exotic, even glamorous, and the familiar and home - grown are humdrum. For specific information there appeared, slowly, a few classic sources to which we could turn: Kipling & King, Brian L.Davis, Mike Chappell, and a very few others. But I could not escape the impression that the subject, overall, was being neglected in print at a time when the collection of these uniforms and pieces of equipment was at last becoming more popular, and prices were still reasonable. When I became a collector myself I soon began to benefit from the generous advice of Richard Ingram; and when he and photographer and fellow collector Martin Brayley began to publish their impressive work in magazine articles, the solution became obvious. We owe them a considerable debt for their heroic expenditure of time and painstaking work.

Since the authors have kindly asked me to write this brief foreword, I intend to indulge myself by explaining why I think this book a worthwhile venture, quite apart from its technical justification as a long-needed reference source for specialist readers. I simply believe that any work which puts younger generations vividly in touch with their forebears of sixty years ago is genuinely valuable: it provides a healthy balance, and encourages a longer, calmer view of today's events.

One of the obvious but slightly shocking discoveries of middle age is that one suddenly notices that increasing numbers of the people one meets do not share memories and attitudes which one had unthinkingly assumed were common to all. When I was born Adolf Hitler was still alive and sending his rockets over my crib on a daily basis; and on a clear day the defences marking the north - western frontier of his continent - wide empire were visible through binoculars from Dover. My boyhood was spent among adults whose everyday lives were almost entirely shaped, for good or ill, by the huge events and inexpressible cost of a very recent world war. Certain important lessons about human behaviour and its consequences were taken for granted as established forever, after immense sacrifices. Now I realise that they have all to be learned again, by every successive generation. Without sounding too pious, let me note one or two of the most important facts about our parents and grandparents of 1939 - 45, who through no choice of their own faced, fought, and finally won the most destructive war in human history.

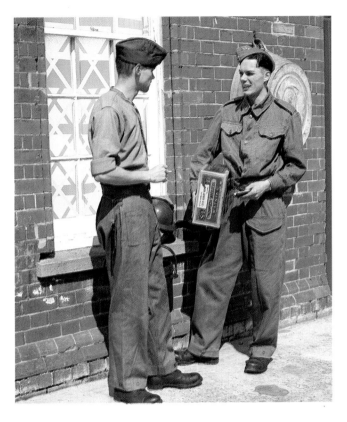

Most nations have had their time in the sun, when circumstances combined to hand them international leadership; this period is usually brief, perhaps a century or so, before the wheels of history turn again. The way in which a country surrenders its power can be as instructive as its behaviour when apparently secure on the peak. With hindsight we can see that Britain's great time was over by 1914, but the fact of her victory in 1918 left her - terribly weakened - with continuing responsibilities. The unmistakable end of global power came with World War II, which left Britain bankrupted and, for the most part, grateful to step back into the second rank once more. But what a way to go - what an honour and privilege! - to give everything in the fight against such enemies; on the right side - for a while, alone on the right side - of perhaps the only undeniably just war in history.

We seem besotted today by "special forces", but that greatest war was not won by any separate warrior caste. The men and women who lived through that enormous experience, and the hundreds of thousands who did not survive it, were almost entirely conscripted civilians; they were us. To an extent seen not even in Nazi Germany, the whole human resources of this country were geared to the battle, and the honour belongs to every single family in Great Britain.

One of our national diseases is obsessive self - criticism; a light attack now and then provides a healthy vaccination, but if it is too deep and prolonged it becomes ugly, dishonest, and ultimately fatal. I hope that this book, in its quiet way, may help act as an antidote.

Martin Windrow

Preface

This book was in the planning stages long before the production of the authors' first joint venture, *World War II British Women's Uniforms*; but for various reasons the Tommy had to wait a while. Now that it is complete we hope that both the beginner and the advanced collector will appreciate the contents. If everyone who reads this book learns at least one new fact that will further their enjoyment and interest then we have achieved at least one of our aims. Although the book has been constructed around the nearly 300 photographs reproduced here, it is planned to be much more than just a "coffee table browser"; the accompanying caption texts are necessarily brief, but we hope that they are both accurately descriptive and informative.

Obviously, we do not pretend to describe in great detail all the items shown - the uniforms, personal equipment and weapons, let alone the vast and only partly recorded field of unit insignia in an obsessively "tribal" army; this book does not set out to be a catalogue. We have tried instead to show original uniforms and other items of kit in plausible combinations for their historical context, recreating the appearance of soldiers of different types at different stages of the war. As with our previous book, all of the uniforms and equipment featured are original to the period portrayed. They have been photographed in a broad variety of realistic scenarios, which we hope present the subjects in a convincing way. We have been at pains to avoid settings which might leave us open to the charge of "glorifying" war; but to have completely omitted battlefield scenarios would have been absurd, denying the purpose behind the development of the items illustrated.

The most obvious limitation is our decision to devote this book solely to the uniforms worn in the European theatre of operations; we hope to cover North Africa, India and the Far East in a future volume. To have included khaki drill and jungle green in this book would have severely limited the diversity of items and depth of detail that could have been shown; and the variety of tropical clothing undoubtedly warrants its own volume. To keep the present work to a manageable and affordable size, and to include as much general issue kit as possible, it has also been necessary to omit many of the developmental and specialist items such as parachutist's equipment, although the basic Airborne Forces kit has been covered here.

(We would also note that in addition to working on KD and JG, we are researching a number of future projects including the uniforms of the Royal Air Force 1935 - 45; not just the glamorous flying clothing, but also the equally important and often overlooked items worn by the "erks" and ground crews.)

The trend toward displaying period uniforms in modern full colour re - creations seems to have been well received by collectors or (as they are termed by the pioneers of this technique, the French magazine *Militaria*) "uniformologists". The term raises the hobby above the level of dignity of the humble browser of dealers' tables at local collectors' fairs, and places it on a par with, say, the numismatists - many of whom would scorn the study of these mundane pieces of hairy serge and canvas webbing. But it is the private collectors who have given the stimulus over recent years to the enormously increased study of uniform history; and that study surely deserves to be taken seriously. The physical realities of the world inhabited by our fathers and grandfathers during the greatest war in history surely deserve careful study and recording; they form an important part of our nation's military heritage.

It is an unavoidable fact that in the immediate aftermath of even the greatest events, the mass - produced clothing and kit of the common soldier is thoughtlessly discarded; and within a few generations museum curators are confronted by the almost complete disappearance of items which were once too common to attract attention, and of any reliable record of how they were worn and used. (A dramatic instance of this is the fact that of all the hundreds of thousands of red jackets issued to the British soldiers of Wellington's armies, less than a dozen are known in the world's public collections today.) We can only hope that as awareness becomes more widespread we will hear fewer stories of thoughtless desecration of the historical record - for instance, sleeves with attractive badge arrays being simply hacked off original World War II battledress blouses by museum staff.... Nobody would be so pompous as to suggest that the preservation of a soldier's jacket is on a par with that of a Wren facade or a Constable landscape; but at its proper level the study of the actual appearance of the citizen soldiers of this uniquely war - torn century surely deserves acknowledgement as a relevant byway of social history.

Whilst we have done our best to ensure that there are no errors in the images or text, any that may be found are the sole responsibility of the authors. Ideally we would like to take all the credit as well, but to do so would belittle the efforts of the many fellow collectors and historians who have supported and encouraged us; the appearance of this book is in no small degree the result of their patience and generosity.

Martin J.Brayley
Richard Ingram
Hampshire
May 1998

Acknowledgements

This venture would not have been possible without the selfless and unstinting assistance of many fellow collectors and friends. We are grateful to them all, from those who lent a single item from their collections to those who were continually on call to answer questions, lend kit, model the uniforms and generally allow themselves to be pestered; and we wish to record our gratitude to, in alphabetical order: Len Andrews, Gary Ashcroft, Neil Ashley, Wayne Batchelor, Gary Bewick, Richard Brace, Lynette Brayley, Charlotte Brayley, Toby Brayley, Steven Brooks, Jason Burnham, Chris Butcher, Mike Carol, WO Peter Carr RM, Cpl "Chappie" Chapple RM, Nick Clarke, Paul Clarke, Nick Comel - Smith, Marcus Cotton, Heber Crawford, Lee Cundick, Chris Davies, Richard Davies, Deborah Draper, Katey Draper, Tony Dudman, Stephanie Dunif, Ian Durrant, Joseph Edmunds, Rod Fleet, Andrew Fletcher, Cpl Jason Garland RM, Jackie Gates, Tom Gates, Martin Gail, Trevor Gail, Andrew Gamblin, Allan Gill, Taff Gillingham, Roger Glancefield, Chris Greenaway, Ben Greening, Nick Hall, Gary Hancock, Barry Hardy, Ralf Harvey, John Haycock, Keith Homer, Alex Hunt, Jason Hunt, Richard Hunt, Will Hutcbings, Isabelle Ingram, James Ingram, Les Jackson, Sgt "JJ" Jennings RM, Mike Johnson, Major Keanen LIR, Richard Knight, Tony Macnamara, Ian Maine, Keith Major, Jon Mills, James Mumford, Linda O'Connel, Cpl Steve Pearce RM, "BJ" Petty, Lawrence Pooley, Allen Prior, Chris Reynolds, James Reynolds, Matt Reynolds, Nick Reynolds, Andrew Robertshaw, Maureen Skellmore, Alex Scott, Phil Slocombe, Bob Stedman, Maurice Stokes, Steve Taylor, Colin Tenn, James Travers, Grant Valentine, Lis Valentine, Simon Van Lint, Alex Webb, Brian Webb, Louise Webb, Molly Web, David Wickens, Suzie Whitehouse, Henry Whitcher, Martin Windrow, Colin Wright.

Aldershot Military Museum, Blunderbuss Antiques, Bolitho Way Solicitors, D - Day Museum, Duke of York's Barracks, Hampshire Constabulary, The Jameson Arms public house, London Irish Rifles, National Army Museum, Portsmouth City Museums, Royal Armouries Fort Nelson, Royal Marines Museum, Sabre Sales, The Tut n' Shive public house.

Section I: From the Phoney War to the Fall of France

The interwar years were relatively peaceful for the British Army, which justified its annual budget by policing the Empire. The apparent worldwide moves towards lasting peace among nations in the exhausted aftermath of the Great War, and deep economic depression, left the military with a low priority and even lower funds. But although often dismissed as a period of stagnation, in reality the late 1920s and the 1930s found the Army looking to the future; despite tight budgets they were developing not only innovative new weapons and equipment, but also new uniforms for the modern soldier.

Between 1902 and 1939 the standard uniform of the British Army was the Service Dress, introduced by Army Orders 10, 40, and 251 of 1902. Originally a loose - fitting and untidy uniform, epitomised by the image of the trench - bound Tommy of the Great War, it was to become during the interwar years one of the smartest uniforms to be worn by the British soldier in the 20th century.

Service dress served the British soldier well; however, by the early 1930s, with an increasing trend toward mechanisation and modernisation, it was thought that a uniform better suited to field use rather than to the parade ground should be developed. Due consideration was given to the current tactical doctrine of rapidly deployable and highly mobile mechanised units; and the search for state - of - the - art weapons for the infantry carried to new levels the increase in platoon, company and battalion firepower which had begun with the adoption of the Lewis light machine gun in 1915. The type of weapons eventually chosen were to have a fundamental effect on the design of the soldier's new kit, perhaps none more so than the Czech ZB30 light machine gun which was eventually accepted into British service in modified form as the "Bren LMG". It was intended to issue the new LMG eventually at the rate of one per eight - man section. This increase in firepower depended upon providing the section with sufficient loaded magazines to keep the ammo - thirsty weapon in action.

Trials of a new Field Service Dress uniform and a new set of cotton webbing equipment took place in the early 1930s. The uniform differed little from the current SD, though improvements included bag - type pockets, open collars and darkened buttons that did not require polishing. Initial trial reports on the web equipment were favourable; but due to ever tighter budgetary constraints it was to be a few more years before any further priority was given to replacing uniforms or equipment.

In 1938 the field service dress re - appeared, but tailored in a lighter denim fabric; and an innovative pattern of field service "overalls" saw limited trials in 1937. The design of this latter uniform owed much to the style of active leisure wear of the period, featuring a short blouson jacket and baggy trousers, as popular with golfers and skiers. This uniform included a Field Service cap rather than the bush - type hat of the earlier trials uniform, thus reviving a design that had first seen widespread issue to the British Army during the late Victorian period. A series of comparison trials found in favour of the overalls, considered to be more comfortable and allowing greater freedom of movement; but it was also considered that the denim fabric used in both uniforms was too light for prolonged field use, and that a heavier, warmer and harder - wearing material should be employed.

At the same time as the new field uniform designs were under consideration a new set of web equipment was undergoing trials. A set of belt, shoulder braces and connectors together with interchangeable components - such as a choice of basic ammunition pouches, smaller cartridge carriers, or a pistol holster and pouch - allowed for systematic adaption of the individual set to suit most arms and services. The emphasis was on its adaptability at infantry section level, where it was essential for the soldier to be able to carry ammunition and magazines for a variety of section and platoon weapons including the LMG, the Boyes anti - tank rifle and the 2 - inch mortar.

Consideration of the trials results eventually led to the adoption of the "overall" pattern, manufactured in khaki wool serge fabric, as the "Battledress, Serge" uniform; the original denim suit was retained only as a fatigue dress. At the same time the new range of webbing was also accepted into service, and became the pattern 1937 web equipment. Thus battledress became the standard uniform of the British soldier of World War II.

On the outbreak of war in September 1939 the British infantryman's greatest handicap lay in the quantity rather than the quality of available equipment. Prime Minister Chamberlain's Munich agreement of September 1938, so widely criticised as a weak act of appeasement, in fact allowed Britain nearly a year in which to increase her preparedness for a continental war - time that was badly needed, and put to good use for the production of weapons and equipment for the British Expeditionary Force which was sent to France. The bitter winter of 1939 - 40 passed uncomfortably but unexcitingly for the BEF; but on 10 May 1940 the Germans' fast - moving *blitzkrieg* offensive burst across the Allied and neutral frontiers, and much of the British Army's new equipment was to be left in France and Belgium as the BEF was driven back to the Channel coast during May and June. In terms of numbers and equipment the British soldier of 1940 did not compare nearly so unfavourably with his German foe as was claimed by the brilliant Nazi propaganda machine; but the Allies' rigid defensive strategy proved quite unequal to the tactical brilliance of the new breed of German generals leading their mechanised spearheads. By mid - June it was all over; some 338,000 British, French, Belgian and Polish troops were evacuated successfully from Dunkirk and other ports, but they arrived in Britain with little more than the clothes they stood up in.

Scottish Troops in Service Dress, 1939

(Left) The Army, faced by some 200,000 mobilised Reservists, Territorials, conscripts and volunteers, is undergoing a hugely expanded recruit training programme. At a Scottish infantry depot an "old sweat" sergeant from the Cameronians (The Scottish Rifles) gives arms training: two young soldiers of the Argyll & Sutherland Highlanders are instructed in the mysteries of the standard platoon anti-tank weapon, the already outdated Boyes 5.5in AT rifle. The bolt-action Boyes was fed by magazines holding a five-round clip, issued in single-pouch cotton bandoliers. It is set down on an early ground sheet/cape, with tan inside and brown rubberised outside surfaces and brass eyelets round the edges. All Scottish units wore the service dress tunic with rounded or cutaway front particular to Scottish troops (and the pipers of some Irish units), and most the Glengarry cap, with the regimental kilt in Highland or trews in Lowland regiments.

(Above) The two young Highland soldiers wear slightly different dress of the day: on the left, the 08 webbing belt with bayonet frog, khaki hose tops, and short puttees - the white, rather than khaki, puttee securing tape is an alternative sometimes worn for added panache. The hose tops and puttees would be replaced for parade and more formal duties by coloured diced hose and white spats, and on such occasions the whitened buff leather belt would also be substituted.

(Right) The sergeant wears the daily working service dress of a Lowland Scottish regiment. The Cameronians, being a Rifle regiment, had the distinction of a rifle green Glengarry with a black toori or tuft, black tunic buttons and badges, and a black leather belt with a white metal snake buckle - the latter normally worn only on ceremonial occasions or perhaps when "walking out". Not illustrated

here are short white spats which could be worn with trews depending on the order of dress. In his right hand the NCO carries a pace stick with which he measures the parade ground. This could be calibrated to the desired length of pace and was used by drill instructors for planning the movements of their men during drill sessions or parades. When folded and tucked under the arm this resplendent device of polished wood and brass also served as an unofficial badge of office

The Glengarry cap was worn - with many varying regimental distinctions - by all Scottish infantry except the Lovat Scouts. The diced band in red and white only is unique to the Argylls, most other regiments wearing dicing of red, white and dark green squares. The black silk badge backing, in cross or bow style, also varies from regiment to regiment, as does the colour of the toori, and even the shape to which the ends of the hanging ribbons are cut.

(Below left) A young private "falls in" in parade order, with buff belt and frog, diced hose, white spats and dress sporran. Note the double collar badges of the amalgamated regiments, and the A&SH shoulder title on the end of his epaulettes. The diced hose varied from regiment to regiment; so did the garter tabs, which at this period were of both coloured puttee tape fabric and felt, and were normally tied around the leg rather than elasticated. On the spats even the buttons and the straps which passed beneath the instep differed in details from one regiment to another.

(Below centre) The full dress sporran - another item whose many detailed variations contributed to the complex uniform distinctions between Scottish regiments. Beneath the brass cantle a shaped piece of black patent leather bears the regimental sporran badge. The Argylls' sporran has six short white tassels mounted in brass cones, earning the regiment the nickname of "the swinging six". These are mounted on leather thongs which pass through eyelets under the hair facing of the main body to fix in the pocket at the rear of the sporran.

The various parts of the sporran are dismountable for cleaning, and this also allows all the different regimental variations to be made up using a limited number of items. This view demonstrates the reason for the cutaway Scottish tunic pattern. The whitened buff strap supporting the sporran is obscured here by the tunic skirt.

(Right) An Argyll awaits his pal as they prepare to walk out; the more showy buff belt and brass GS locket buckle are worn with the undress sporran. In dimpled brown leather with a matching strap and the regimental sporran badge on the front, this is much less ostentatious than the full dress counterpart. The Argylls' kilt was in the dark blue, dark green and black 42nd (Government) sett - and note the pin. This particular regiment was distinguished by box pleats at the rear of the kilt, but in the face of wartime demand kilts of the standard design would also have been issued.

(Below right) Detail of labelling of Scottish other ranks' service dress tunic, c.1939.

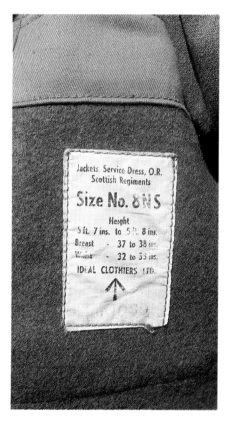

Prewar Dress Blues & Denim Fatigues

(Below) As the BEF began to arrive in France and Belgium in the late autumn of 1939 their immediate task was consolidation of defences. Dressed in the old prewar denim fatigue uniform with the new khaki serge FS cap, this private in the Royal Berkshires makes his first contribution to the war effort with a General Service shovel. During this early period there is photographic evidence of both the new denim battledress and the old working dress being worn side by side; new stocks would not be issued until the old garments had been used up and worn out. The denim fabric has a distinctive brown colouring which fades with washing and wear. The jacket is of simple cut without exterior breast pockets, and fastens with five small removable GS buttons with brass rings holding them at the rear through the shank. The trousers are cut the same as service dress trousers, rising to a V - shape at the rear; the braces and fly buttons are of brass dished type. Even on fatigues gas masks are carried.

(Above & above right) Jacket and Trousers, Serge, Blue, OR, or more simply "blues" were worn as full dress (classed as No 1 dress for mounted units and No 2 dress for dismounted) with the appropriate regimental headdress or the coloured pattern stiff SD cap. The uniform was also worn for walking out with the coloured FS cap; in many regiments blues were the standard "Sunday best" uniform. Sergeants, and corporals of Foot Guards, were allowed to carry a bayonet frogged to a white buff belt of Slade Wallace pattern when walking out. Waistbelts were not to be worn by other ranks, but this ruling was often ignored.

Here a Territorial soldier from The Duke of Wellington's Regiment (West Riding) enjoys a pint at his local pub in the weeks before he is mobilised and shipped to France with the BEF. The tunic and trousers were made from heavy, rather rough wool serge, tailored to a close fit; the trousers had a raised back section, as found on khaki SD trousers of the period, and the scarlet - piped legs had a distinct taper towards the ankle, the cuff of which was cut at an angle sloping to the rear. This uniform is marked "7

DWR"; regulations demanded that it should bear the title of the Regiment or Corps above the soldier's regimental number above the month and year of issue, but few uniforms issued in the 1930s bear full regulation markings. Regimental collar badges were worn, as were small size (24 - 34 line) regimental buttons. On the epaulettes the brass titles show T over DW; previously Territorial battalion numerals had also been worn, but these were discontinued, to be followed soon afterwards by the Territorial T following the full mobilisation of Territorial forces in 1939. The stand or "mandarin" collar was lined, but was still notably uncomfortable.

Following the outbreak of war some units turned in their blues and buff belts for salvage. The brass buttons and badges were removed as were the belt fittings; the leather work was burnt or otherwise disposed of and the wool was recycled into more useful items such as Army blankets. This practice was most common among overseas units returning to the UK; shipping space was at a premium and it was easier to dispose of surplus equipment in theatre.

Service Dress, 1939

(Above) A Regular private of The Royal Berkshire Regiment, who has yet to receive the new battledress uniform, prepares to leave the barracks on a Sunday afternoon. He displays the service dress of the interwar soldier complete with regimental shoulder titles, buttons and collar badges. For walking out and for occasional ceremonial duties the 1888 pattern whitened buff leather belt was retained by certain units, with the universal brass locket buckle. The inverted chevron at the base of the left sleeve is a good conduct stripe for three years' exemplary service.

(Above right) Even by September 1939 battledress uniform had yet to reach all serving Regulars, let alone the Territorials, Reservists, conscripted Militia, or the flood of willing volunteers. Here a Reservist recalled on the eve of war has been re-issued with the soon to be obsolete uniform of his previous service with the colours. Only his boots with toe-cap welts and his respirator haversack distinguish this significantly from his father's uniform of 1914-18; his new tunic from the stores has yet to sport even its collar badges or regimental buttons – in this case those of The Middlesex Regiment.

(Right) Mounted service dress. The demise of service dress following the outbreak of war would spell the virtual end of the OR's breeches worn by mounted units, so this Royal Artillery gunner marks the end of an era. The SD tunic is the same as worn by dismounted troops, although some cavalry units had the collars tailored to a stand or mandarin pattern in place of the normal stand-and-fall shape. The twill breeches, with reinforced seat and inner thighs, are worn with long puttees wound in the reversed manner adopted by mounted troops. Some units would retain as late as 1941 the leather bandolier which had formed part of the 1903 mounted equipment, and which was also used by the Royal Signals as part of their service dress. The loss of such a smart uniform in favour of the practical battledress was to break the heart of many a sergeant major. The use of the Royal Artillery's flaming grenade as a "collar dog" was soon to cease, but it would be retained for use on the FS and the later GS caps; it was felt that the RA's gun badge was too large for the FS cap (although both badges were in fact to be seen worn on it). The Royal Artillery's white regimental lanyard would continue to be worn by gunners on their battledress.

Early Officer's Service Dress

(Left) Dating back to major uniform changes in 1902, the officer's SD uniform varied in detail from regiment to regiment despite attempts to introduce a universal pattern. Prior to World War II the tunic had a distinct flare to the lower skirts and had been worn slightly longer; by 1939 the flare and the length had both been reduced, although the older patterns were still to be seen. As a mounted officer this captain of Royal Artillery

wears the Breeches, Mounted Pattern worn by all ranks of mounted units and by mounted officers of dismounted units. These were popular early in the war but were gradually replaced by the more functional trousers introduced in 1933, which had generally been worn off duty. The Sam Browne belt was worn with the SD tunic; from the left shoulder of his early pattern tunic this staff officer wears a whistle on a lanyard; his service respirator hangs on his left hip; and he carries documents in a War Department briefcase bearing the royal cypher of King George VI. The carriage of a cane was popular during this period, although the practice declined during the war.

(Inset) Boots, Mounted Officers, a high field boot with a three - buckle gaiter - style top and a laced instep. This is the standard pattern; as with much officers' kit variations were seen, including a fully laced pattern which was not particularly popular. Spurs were worn or not depending upon duties, though it was quite common to see "desk warriors" still wearing them - pomp overcoming practicality.

(Far right) Royal Artillery officers of coastal defence and mechanised units were required to wear the Breeches, Knickerbocker of dismounted officers; these "plus fours" were very popular during the 1930s, but rapidly fell into disuse after the outbreak of war. Short legged and of very full cut, they were styled on civilian golfing trousers of the period. They were worn with puttees and regulation brown leather ankle boots (black in Rifle regiments). The flare of the skirt on the early tunic illustrated here is more pronounced than on wartime manufactured

examples. The chinstrap on the service dress cap is of a narrow prewar pattern - they became somewhat wider on wartime production caps.

(Inset) Officer's brown leather ankle boots. Minor variations in style were to be encountered in all officers' items purchased privately to basic recommended patterns; the leeway enjoyed by individuals depended upon wealth, taste, and the tolerance of their regimental adjutants. Note the fullness of the knickerbocker breeches; the fall of fabric over the knee was not supposed to exceed four inches.

Battledress, Serge, 1939

(Above) Battledress was an innovative concept in its day, the most modern and rational combat uniform adopted by any European power. It was more economical than the old long tunics worn by other armies; and a great deal of thought had gone into its design, down to the level of exactly what could be carried in which pockets. Production of the original pattern of BD, often erroneously called 1937 pattern, started in 1938, but issue in quantity did not begin until 1939. Typically, this soldier in early 1939 has been issued the new BD but has yet to receive the 1937 pattern web equipment; he makes do with 1908 pattern, identical to that issued during the Great War except for the entrenching tool and its helve, which had been discarded during the interwar period. All buttons on the BD were of the concealed "fly" type; they were normally of dished brass, with the exception of those for the epaulettes which were soon replaced by composition buttons with a metal shank.

(Top right) Widely issued for wear with the new BD was the universal pattern khaki Field Service (FS) cap. Unlike the stiff visored SD cap which it largely replaced, this had the advantage that it could easily be folded and stored in a pack or pocket, or tucked under an epaulette. This cap bears on the left front of the body the badge of The Devonshire Regiment, of prewar metal manufacture. Although it was never intended that the prewar brass epaulette titles should be worn on BD this practice was commonplace when the uniform was first issued, adding a touch of sparkle to an otherwise unrelievedly drab appearance.

(Centre right) Rear of the 1908 webbing set.

(Right) Our private of the Devonshires, not yet issued with the Anklets, Web, of the 37 pattern set, makes use of the small straps let into the inside of each ankle section of the Trousers, Battledress, Serge. These could be drawn around the ankle and fastened using one of two buttons, to confine the bulk of fabric with the intention of improving the fit of the web anklets. At his feet lies the Mk I* steel helmet in use at this time; it consisted of a Mk I helmet shell - the old 1916 Brodie pattern - fitted from 1936 with an improved liner (note oval rubber pad in skull) and an elasticated web chinstrap. This pattern was not fully superseded by the Mk II until late 1940.

Single - breasted & 1939 Pattern Greatcoats

(Left) *Our recalled Reservist of The Middlesex Regiment is dressed in an old pattern single - breasted great-coat, typical of the older items released from stores to equip the vastly expanded numbers of men in khaki. Single-breasted greatcoats were beginning to be phased out in 1939 in favour of a new double - breasted pattern; this particular example is of earlier interwar man-ufacture, as identified by the rein-forced "rifle patches" on the shoul-ders. At the rear the coat has a half - belt adjustable for tightness with three buttons, of General Service type on this example. Like the SD tunic, greatcoats came from the Quartermaster with GS buttons which might then be exchanged for regimental patterns at unit level.*

(Below) *The new 1939 pattern double - breasted greatcoat for other ranks, worn here by a sergeant in The Royal Sussex Regiment. As pre-scribed, he displays on both sleeves rank chevrons of the type worn on service dress and battledress - khaki backing with stripes of white her-ringbone pattern. The epaulettes bear temporary slip - on titles; offi-cially the only regimental identifica-tion permitted to be worn on uni-form by line infantry and cavalry regiments and most corps in the early part of the war, these replaced brass shoulder titles. Simple khaki cloth patches with a tape loop to fit under the epaulette, they were stitched in black with the title e.g. R.SUSSEX.*

(Left) Rear views of interwar single - breasted and (right) double - breasted 1939 pattern greatcoats worn over SD and BD respectively. Note the expansion pleat up the back of the older pattern, and the three - button half - belt for adjustment. The 1939 pattern has a buttoned lower vent but no pleat in the upper back. It does have a half - belt, but here the two ends of the belt have been tucked inside the coat through two slots at the outer ends. This allows the greatest expansion of the back for wearing extra layers of clothing or equipment underneath the coat.

(Below) General view of the pockets and interior detail of the 1939 coat. This is also a good angle to make out details of the FS cap, which was supposed to be worn with the front above the right eye. Note the crown, body, peak and curtain sections, the latter fixed by two small front buttons and with its highest points hooked to eyelets in the sides of the body.

(Above & right) A day of changeable weather in spring 1940, somewhere in France; two officers of the BEF wear (left) the traditionally popular "British warm", and (right) the officers' regulation greatcoat - both privately purchased off the peg or, more often than not, individually tailored. The British warm was purchased either as an individual choice or because it was fashionable amongst the officers of particular units. It was available commercially in a variety of fabrics and shades. It is shorter than the greatcoat, and does not necessarily close fully across at the collar; generally it is a more tailored garment, not designed to expand to fit over equipment, with lining throughout and stylish features such as an open - top left breast pocket and sometimes cuff buttons. Typical of its more casual style are the leather "football" buttons fitted to this example.

The long Greatcoat, Universal Pattern worn by the right hand officer is double - breasted, in a smooth melton or doeskin fabric; the cut remains essentially unchanged since before the Great War; the lapels can be closed at the throat or worn open. Internally the back is only half lined; the side pockets are often lined with a soft moleskin fabric; and the cuffs, originally for turning down over the hands in cold weather, are by now ornamental. Rank insignia are worn on the epaulettes in bronze or gilt finish; buttons are always regimental officers' pattern with stiff shanks - those on the left front are "plugged" (set into the fabric so that they sit flat). By the end of the war the Army was providing an officer's greatcoat for purchase from the Quartermaster. Other ranks' greatcoats were sometimes retailored commercially to the officer's pattern.

(**Above**) May 1940: the speed of the German advance and the streams of refugees who took to the roads to escape it caused chaos. From an improvised office in a French farm-yard part of an infantry company headquarters try to deal with requests for help and information as the tide of uprooted humanity floods westwards; they themselves will probably be on the move again soon. Communication between the company and battalion HQ depends on land lines, and this field telephone exchange is handling these calls; the lieutenant in the foreground is try-ing to contact his MT officer using the Tele F handset. In the left waist of his greatcoat note the slot through which the sword hilt protruded when it was worn for ceremonial duties from a belt beneath the coat.

(**Right**) An officer wearing a pri-vately purchased trenchcoat. The most popular brand was Burbery; this example is a more modestly priced version from C.Montague Burton, but has all the features tra-ditional since the Great War (see also page 69) - double - breasted cut with storm back and shoulders, inte-gral belt with D - rings, and but-toned on epaulettes. Such coats would have been purchased at the officer's discretion according to which pattern or brand was favoured by the unit in which he served.

Stretcher bearers, 51st (Highland) Division, France 1940

(*Left & below*) All regiments and corps had a number of other ranks trained as stretcher bearers and first aiders; King's Regulations (paragraph 816a) stated that in infantry battalions, as a minimum, the band sergeant, band corporal and 20 bandsmen, with a reserve of four men, were to fulfil this role, and additional numbers could qualify if time and instructors permitted. Kilted Highland regiments were ordered into battledress in September 1939; the kilt was unsuitable for modern war, and maintaining supplies would have been very expensive (a kilt with its accessories cost £4, BD trousers only 11s 4d - about 57p). However, photographs taken during the early campaign in France show some continued use of the kilt, particularly by pipers and bandsmen, and thus by stretcher bearers. The kilt was worn protected by a tan cover, as used here, or a simple apron of the same fabric; both had a small "sporran"

pocket at the front.

Here a Highland stretcher bearer, identified by his brassard, attends to a wounded ally - a French brigadier - chef *of* Chasseurs à cheval *serving with a Divisional Reconnaissance Group is given a drink and a lighted cigarette before he is evacuated to the rear areas. He is still clutching his ANP 31 gas mask, but has dumped the rest of his kit. This burly Jock shows off the front and side views of the Mk I* helmet with its 1916 - shape shell, subtly different from the Mk II and typical for the period.*

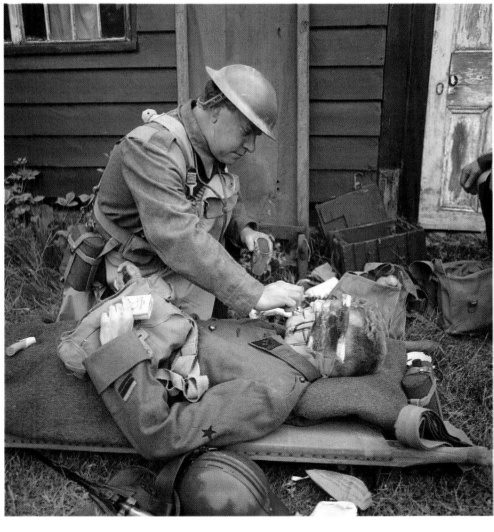

(Above) Some of the weight of the stretchered casualty is distributed by the use of a harness looped over the stretcher handles and around the bearer's neck; this also helped prevent the patient being dropped should the bearer lose his grip or stumble. Note clear view of kilt cover.

(Right) Battalion stretcher bearers often wore pistol belt order and carried an Enfield or similar .38 revolver, since they did not enjoy the same non - combatant status as members of the Royal Army Medical Corps and other regular medical and nursing services. The pistol lanyard is worn here in the prescribed manner, which was awkward when it had to pass over a respirator worn at the ready position, and could easily get snagged or grabbed.

(Bottom right) Shell dressing bag; dating back to the Great War, this was used only for basic medical items such as field dressings. Its designation was stencilled on the top flap, above the international sign of a red cross on a white disc painted on the satchel body.

BEF Infantry, France 1940

(Left) As the BEF is pushed back to the French coast in May 1940 an infantryman (who also appears on the front cover of this book) waits for orders, with rifle slung. Although not yet issued to the BEF in its entirety, the battledress uniform in its original specification as manufactured from late 1938 was in use with most front line units; note the uncomfortable unlined collar of the serge blouse. A Mk VI respirator haversack carries the gas mask in the alert position; this particular model was introduced in 1939. Passing through the rings of the respirator haversack are the white tapes of the Cape, Anti - Gas, seen rolled behind the soldier's head and resting above his small pack. A hessian cover with additional "brush loops" is fitted over the Mk II helmet (manufactured from 1938) to camouflage it and prevent reflections. Such covers, echoing practice during the Great War, were unofficial but were made up by certain units during the battle of France; one original example is known with a painted hessian divisional flash sewn on. Helmet nets were also beginning to be issued and saw limited use in France; but most helmets were worn uncovered and uncamouflaged - which is somewhat surprising, as the paint finish on many early helmets was "eggshell" or satin rather than matt, without the addition of sand to coarsen the finish and kill reflections. Note that this respirator haversack has been "blancoed" - scrubbed with the same water - dilute powder preservative as the webbing harness. Later in the war hessian covers were sometimes seen worn over haversacks to prevent heavy soiling during exercises; the haversack could not easily be laundered without appearing conspicuously washed out thereafter.

(Below left)
Detail of first pattern battledress trousers, the field dressing pocket on the right hip with a single expansion pleat and no button. The low position of the basic pouches identifies them as the Mk I version, with belt attachment hooks positioned relatively high on the rear. Some early pouches have three loops sewn to the underside of the flap, supposedly so that the soldier could keep separate from his ball rounds a few ballistite cartridges for use with the grenade discharger cup. The Mk I pouch ceased manufacture in 1940.

(Far left & left) As part of the rethink of most of the soldier's equipment taking place at the end of the 1930s, some troops in France had on trial a new entrenching tool, a departure from the 1908 pick/mattock model which had drifted out of use between the wars. A short spade tool as used by the French, Germans and most other European armies, it was officially a part of the 37 pattern equipment; it began manufacture in 1939 but was never universally issued. Ordinarily seen in use by infantry only, it disappeared after 1941 with the re - adoption of the previous pattern. A carrier for this implement also exists as part of the short - lived 1939 leather equipment.

The 1939 entrenching tool was carried in a web cover on the left hip; here the scabbard of the bayonet for the SMLE No 1 Mk III rifle has been passed through the securing strap of the cover to cut down the flapping and clattering when on the move. The long wooden handle hanging well below the belt line was awkward, and it is easy to see why this new design did not prove popular. One original photograph shows troops marching back through France in May 1940 wearing only the covers, the tools presumably having been discarded.

(Above) View of 37 pattern small pack, officially termed the haversack, slung behind the shoulders on the detachable L-shaped shoulder straps which hooked to the basic pouches at the front; the pack could thus be dropped with ease, not being an integral part of the harness. The same L - straps were used with the large pack; when this was carried as part of Field Service Marching Order the haversack was attached to the brace ends on the left hip. Here an early brown ground sheet/cape is tucked under the flap. According to the manual the haversack was to contain the woollen pullover jersey next to the back, and in its outer divided compartments the mess tins (of a new pattern), cutlery, emergency ration, and - surprisingly - the water bottle; in reality this is always seen worn suspended on the webbing. The anti - gas cape rests above the haversack ready to be unfolded if required. This example of the anti - gas cape is of typical green "tacky" fabric treated with linseed oil; other early war examples are in a light tan "non - tacky" material. The blue and white enamelled tin mug hangs from the haversack strap ready for a brew - up at a moment's notice.

A brief rest during the long fighting retreat to Dunkirk in May - June 1940 finds BEF infantrymen and French refugees mixed by the roadside. The word has been passed permitting these Regulars to drink from their water bottles. In order to do this the bottle and its carrier have been unbuckled together from the right side of the webbing equipment: the bottle is difficult to remove from the tight - fitting carrier, and even more difficult to replace without the help of a mate. Note that the battledress blouses are absolutely bare of unit insignia. By the spring of 1940 only a few unofficial battalion sleeve flashes, along similar lines to the "battle badges" of 1916 - 18, had begun to come into use with the BEF. These were usually simple coloured felt shapes - bars, strips, capbadge silhouettes, etc. - adopted at battalion level; only 51st (Highland) Division seems to have had an organised system, and even that was not universally seen. With the return of the BEF from Dunkirk its troops were reorganised, and these battle patches disappeared.

Despatch Rider, France 1940

April 1940: a BEF "Don R", his corps identified by the white and blue Royal Signals brassard, sits astride his Norton 16H and opens a map board to check his position at a French crossroads. At the beginning of the war the Army motorcyclist's protective wet weather gear comprised this short double - breasted coat, leggings, and motorist type helmet in khaki rubberised cotton fabric, together with goggles and gauntlets. The waterproof coat, of approximately mid - thigh length, had a double - breasted front secured with plastic dished buttons; behind the closure was an extra storm flap, and pieces of elasticated fabric secured the inside of the wrists. The map board in use here during the early part of the war has a wooden base and a canvas flap with pencil and ruler pockets; this is held fastened by a number of press studs, and the maps inside are secured by two khaki elasticated cotton tapes passing over a perspex cover. There is a carrying handle at the rear.

(Right) Detail of helmet and teardrop - shaped MT goggles; the helmet owes much to prewar civilian models, and gives protection only from the elements. Note the ear flaps secured with press studs, presumably so that they could be unfastened when in conversation; and the adjustment strap across the forehead. The chin strap engages the buckle on the right flap. The white cotton fleece lining is just visible where the left flap is lifting. The rear of the helmet is elasticated to hold it in securely against the nape.

(Below) Gaiter - style fastening of the leggings, which taper in at the ankle and extend over the laced instep of the boot; note the buckled leather strap passing under the instep. Inside the button fastening is folded an extra swathe of fabric which allows enough expansion when the legging is being put on or taken off. At the top the leggings have straps of the same material which button round a belt supporting them at the waist; the tops are cut with the front high and sloping down towards the rear. There also exist Leggings, Rubberised, 1A, manufactured from some time in 1941. These are a pair of rubberised overtrousers with the same gaiter leg arrangement

and with built - in braces. They may perhaps have been issued to motorcyclists, but were basically an item of wet weather clothing on general issue with the Coat 1A (see page 50) to other transport drivers or personnel who had to function in wet weather, such as Military Police.

(Below right) Home service, early 1941: the first pattern "pulp" helmet, so named because its shell was made from a composite of paper and rag. Introduced from the end of 1939, this was the first proper protective helmet to be sanctioned by the Army, and was initially for issue only to despatch riders and MP motorcyclists. It is worn here by an old sweat of the Royal Corps of Signals: note slip - on R.SIGNALS title, and three good conduct stripes denoting 12 years' exemplary service. Note the leather neck flap and chin strap arrangement with press stud closure of the ear flaps. An economy version manufactured from August 1940 was made from a compressed rubber and fibre compound; it is distinguishable by the absence of the two reinforcing bands passing round the edge of this shell above and below the liner attachment lace.

Iceland 1940

The extreme conditions encountered in this posting demanded the issue of specialised clothing. The "Snow and Mountain" scales of issue included everything needed to retain body heat, including such items as thick woollen socks, balaclavas, scarves and mittens - often supplemented by "comforts" items knitted by families and organisations such as the Women's Institute. The basic cold weather outer garment early in the war was the "Tropal" coat; early patterns were sheepskin - lined, but as this expensive material was in great demand for various other items of military clothing, particularly for aircrews, it was later replaced with the cheaper and only marginally less efficient kapok.

The ankle - length Coat, Sheepskin, made to a pattern dating back to the Great War, provided a good degree of protection. The heavy canvas outer had a waterproof interlining and an insulating upper body lining of sheepskin. Elasticated inner cuffs and a large serge collar provided wrist and neck seals; the front was secured by five metal clip fasteners. The replacement Coat, Kapok Lined was externally identical at first, but the metal clips were later replaced by wooden toggles and cord loops.

Balaclavas and woollen scarves were issued in many theatres, the full face and head protection offered by combining the two being most welcome in Iceland's sub - arctic winter (this photograph was taken at minus 40 degrees C).

(Right) The sheepskin winter cap had a fleece peak and side curtains, the latter being worn either down to protect the ears or turned up against the body of the hat. The exterior was made of white or khaki wool serge, with a quilted fabric lining.

(Below) Gloves, Woollen - a general issue item, supplemented in colder climates with woollen mittens. Although providing better insulation these reduced the dexterity needed for many tasks. The metal spring clips on the early coats were easier to operate with gloved hands than the loops and wooden toggles that replaced them, which often obliged men to remove their gloves.

(Left) While providing adequate insulation for those on static duties, the coat's bulk and weight made its use for active tasks impractical. The wearer soon overheated even in severe cold, leading to sweat condensing on the lining; this soon froze, drastically reducing the coat's insulating properties and leading to rapid loss of body heat and consequent cold - related injuries.

Manufacturers often labelled the kapok coats as sheepskin; this is typical of the wartime overlap of production labelling frequently encountered on clothing. Old labels were used up even though specifications had changed, and apparently contradictory labelling has often puzzled collectors.

Section II: The Long Road Back

In the summer and autumn of 1940 the British Army - with adequate manpower and small arms, but desperately short of artillery, armour and anti - tank weapons - was preoccupied with the threat of German invasion. Victory in the aerial Battle of Britain was followed by the Luftwaffe's night bombing campaign on British cities, and relentless U - boat attacks on our ocean lifelines. After a year facing the Axis alone (with the honourable exception of Greece) the German invasion of Russia in June 1941 at least brought Britain the comfort of a major fighting ally in what was clearly going to be a grinding war of attrition.

From 1941 to 1944 British armies faced the Axis overseas on the battlefields of North Africa, Malaya, Burma, Sicily, and later Italy. The lessons of all these campaigns fed into the vast and often cumbersome machinery that clothed and equipped the Army which was evolving in readiness for the return to mainland Europe. At the level of the individual soldier's kit three main factors are identifiable.

Firstly, the battledress uniform and 37 pattern webbing equipment absorbed a number of adaptations as initial flaws were ironed out in the light of combat experience. The abrasive blouse collar was lined with khaki drill fabric; the hip field dressing pocket acquired an extra expansion pleat and a button. The basic ammunition pouches were moved higher on the belt; even before Dunkirk webbing cross straps and L - shaped pack straps appeared with narrow and broad sections stitched together rather than woven in one piece; 1941 saw the first issue of a much simplified sleeve - type waterbottle carrier; and the canvas anklet straps, which had a tendency to work loose, were replaced with leather.

Secondly, the massive pressure on financial and all other national resources led to measures to economise on materials and production time. The Army's battledress appeared in a "utility" version, often labelled as the 1940 pattern (although production did not begin until well into 1941 or issue until 1942). The front, pocket and cuff buttons were no longer concealed by fly flaps; breast pocket pleats and trouser leg tightening tabs were dispensed with. The denim working uniform underwent the same austerity modifications as its serge counterpart. This process of simplifying and thus cheapening production would continue steadily. From 1943, to reduce the quantity of brass used on web equipment, brass end tags were omitted from the attachment straps on small and large packs and the shoulder sections of the L - straps. The brass plate securing the belt adjustment hooks was replaced by stiching, and the brass keeps each side of the buckle by web loops. Web cross straps and L - straps were further modified at the point where the broad shoulder section met the narrow section, the broad end now being folded under and stitched to avoid unecessary finishing work. Finally, from 1944 brass fittings began to be replaced altogether by gunmetal.

Thirdly, the raising and expansion of specialist branches of the Army was to see the manufacture and development of completely new items of uniform and equipment to meet their particular requirements. The main examples were the wide ranges of kit introduced for Airborne Forces and mountain troops; the appearance of camouflage clothing both in mimetic patterns and for use in snow; and the gradual development of practical clothing for armoured vehicle crews and motorcyclists.

Throughout the period 1941 - 44 the British soldier could be seen struggling against the official tendency to submerge him and his unit in an anonymous khaki mass. The wearing of coloured field service caps was followed first by tolerated regimental sleeve flashes, and then by official divisional patches from late 1940. Although coloured regimental and corps shoulder titles were not universally authorised until 1943, this merely recognised an existing situation arising from the determined esprit de corps of many individual units; the British Army has, after all, been built on "tribal" loyalties since the 17th century. This urge perhaps had its most obvious expression when the Army Clothing Department was authorised to supply special coloured berets for the new, elite Airborne and Commando units, thus starting a military fashion which has since been copied worldwide.

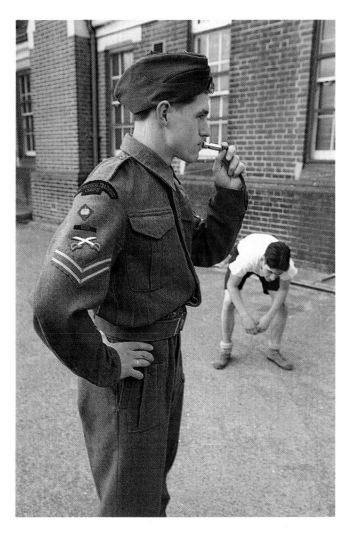

A corporal instructor of the Army Physical Training Corps – see also page 52.

Hospital Blues

Soldiers staying in military hospitals or convalescent homes were issued hospital blue uniform. This consisted of a white shirt with attached collar; a red tie; and a bright blue serge waistcoat, trousers and tunic. Early manufacture tunics had a white facing to the lapel fronts, a carry - over from World War I issue. The hospital blue uniform was much disliked by those who had to wear it; often the jacket was dispensed with in favour of the battle-dress blouse worn with the blue trousers, white shirt and red tie. In this way rank, formation badges and medal ribbons were displayed for all to see.

(Right) In keeping with the fashion of the day a waistcoat was issued to patients as part of what was essentially a civilian cut three - piece suit; it had two small waist pockets. Like the other hospital blue garments it was unlined, and the quality of the wool serge was poorer than normally expected for military uniform. Obscured here, the white shirt had a full length front opening fastened with gunmetal buttons - this was to avoid possible strain on injured limbs and wounds in putting on and taking off the Army's normal half - buttoned pullover shirt. No special headwear was issued with the hospital blues; this prewar Regular of The Royal Warwickshire Regiment retains his old SD cap.

(Below) The rear view of the waistcoat shows its adjustable tie tape and high back. The jacket had a short central vent in the lower part of the full length back seam.

(Opposite) The blue jacket was of a simple design, with a four - button front and two open - top skirt pockets. Only a limited size range was available, with most garments having an adjustment tie at the waist; typically trousers were either too long or too short in the leg. However, these simply adjustable garments also allowed for the relief of any pressure on wounds, as well as providing a wider size range in a single item of clothing. This convalescent soldier of The Oxfordshire & Buckinghamshire Light Infantry wears his khaki FS cap for a little light exer-cise in the grounds of a military hospital on the arm of a nursing sister; in bad weather soldiers wore their issue greatcoat with a hospital blue sleeve armlet. A member of the Queen Alexandra's Imperial Military Nursing Service (Reserve), the sister wears the early pattern lancer - fronted ward dress, and has her badge of office (not a medal) pinned to the right corner of her tippet. Sister was the basic QAIMNS(R) rank, equivalent to lieutenant; note the two rank stars (in everyday language, "pips") worn on the shoulders.

RTR Tank Crewman, 1941

(Left) This trooper wears the most distinctive item issued to the Royal Tank Regiment: the black beret, copied from those worn in 1918 by the French chasseurs alpins, and finally approved by King George V in March 1924. The RTR cap badge bearing the scroll "Fear Naught" dates from 1922. Note the RTR slip - on title at the base of the BD blouse epaulette. The use of the black beret, with individual regimental badges, was extended to the whole of the Royal Armoured Corps in 1940; in practice many cavalry regiments seem to have kept the FS cap into 1942.

(Below left) The long strap holster was designed specifically for AFV crews; it was believed that positioning the holster at mid - thigh allowed easier access to the weapon for men working in the confines of an armoured vehicle. In practice the extra long strap frequently snagged on the many obstructions inside the tank, making the design unpopular with crews.

(Below) The unsuitable long strap holster was eventually altered to allow it to be worn at waistbelt level. Note the differing shades of khaki blanco on this belt and holster, due to weathering of the holster and extra applications to the belt when worn alone. The holster had six web cartridge loops stitched to its face, but ammunition was usually carried in a pouch which offered better protection; a stitched tube at the front held the cleaning rod.

(Bottom) The pouch was normally worn on the left side of the belt with the holster on the right, but at individual preference it could also be fitted over the top of the holster belt loop. The Enfield No 2 Mk I* .38 revolver, introduced in 1938, had no hammer spur in order to avoid snagging and accidental discharge inside the tank. Since it therefore had to be fired double - action - i.e. by prolonged pressure on the trigger without first cocking the hammer - this ensured that there was little or no chance of the average trooper hitting anything. The tank crewman's pistol was generally agreed to be an almost wholly useless item; a sub - machine gun was later stowed in the turret for use by dismounted crewmen.

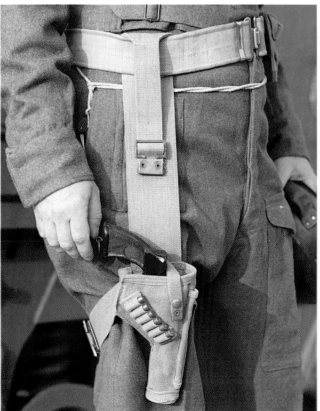

The Royal Tank Regiment traced its lineage back to the Tank Corps formed in 1917, which became the Royal Tank Corps in 1923. The gradual development of the concept of mechanised warfare during the 1920s and 1930s saw the parallel mechanisation of the horsed cavalry - at first slowly and piecemeal, but rapidly from 1935. In April 1939 the Royal Armoured Corps was formed, comprising the Household and line cavalry and the RTC; the latter was now retitled Royal Tank Regiment. Like the Royal Regiment of Artillery, the RTR was in fact a corps comprising several numbered battalions, later confusingly retitled regiments - e.g. 1st Royal Tank Regiment, 2nd Royal Tank Regiment, etc.; during the war 23 numbered RTR regiments saw service. For tactical purposes the RTR and armoured cavalry regiments were deployed within Armoured Brigades in Armoured Divisions; or within Tank Brigades, which were independent assets available to Army, Corps or Divisional commanders mainly for infantry support. The large numbers of tank units required by the climax of the war were provided partly by raising six new cavalry regiments, and partly by converting infantry battalions to the armoured role as numbered regiments of the RAC - e.g. 5th Battalion, The King's Own Royal Regiment (Lancaster) became 107th Regiment RAC.

(Right) *Crash Helmet, RTR - a 1939 modification of the original 1936 pattern of protective helmet. This helmet was distinctive in that it had a multi - piece construction to the crown covering, and rubber grommets in the ventilation holes. This type of headgear offered protection only from the plentiful knocks and bumps suffered by crewmen inside moving tanks; it gave no ballistic protection whatsoever.*

(Below) *Crash Helmet, RAC - a hard fibre helmet which first saw widespread issue in 1941. As with the earlier pattern, increased protection in the form of a padded section was added to the most vulnerable point at the front. Barely visible on the left side of this green - painted example is a red, yellow and green triangular flash of the 5th Royal Inniskilling Dragoon Guards. The maker's label inside is marked with the number 7, by Helmets Ltd of Wheathampstead, dated 1941.*

(Above) *Side view of Crash Helmet, RAC. Many were fitted with a side curtain which allowed the fitting of earphones; this example is wired with receivers for the WS19, a 15 watt armoured force wireless set having a range of between 10 and 20 miles.*

Anti - Gas Equipment, 1941

(Opposite) Shown here is the Cape, Anti - Gas in an uncamouflaged version; it was also issued in a cloud pattern of green and brown. The title is confusing, since it is not a cape but a sleeved overcoat, introduced as part of the modernisation programme of the late 1930s - when all major armies were seriously concerned that the poison gases of which they had such bitter memories from 1915 - 18 would be widely used on the modern battlefield. Made from treated cotton fabric, its purpose was to protect the wearer from corrosive liquid gases delivered in the form of an air - spray; these would penetrate ordinary clothing and burn the skin beneath. Eyeshields, Anti - Gas were to prevent the soldier from being blinded by liquid gas; here a pair are worn in the alert position on the helmet.

These came in a pack of six and were carried in a pocket of the respirator haversack. Greater protection from liquid or vapour gases was provided by the full face respirator. The remaining exposed areas of skin such as the hands and neck would be immediately treated with Ointment, Anti - Gas; this came in tubes in a tin box kept in a pocket inside the respirator haversack, or in the pocket on the outside of the cape. The cape is of voluminous cut, to accomodate the webbing equipment; to prevent overheating there are three large ventilation holes under each arm. Our soldier is on gas picket at a heightened state of alert, with his respirator at the ready and holding a gas rattle with which to sound the alarm.

(Above) The "humped" back was shaped to fit over the soldier's pack.

(Above right) Detail of eyeshields, and respirator haversack worn in the alert position.

(Right) Cape and respirator being worn with the Helmet Cover & Curtain, Anti - Gas. Note also the pocket on the cape for carrying a tin of ointment or a gas detection kit. The bottom front corners of the cape opening have press studs allowing the skirts to be fixed back for easier movement on the march - see opposite.

(Right) Detail of anti - gas helmet cover (uncamouflaged - again, examples with cloud - pattern camouflage are known), and early service box respirator face piece and hose. This is an improved version of the anti - gas helmet curtain for protecting the back and sides of the head; as introduced in 1940 the curtain was fixed only to the rim of the helmet, without an overall cover. The cape, cover and anti - gas gauntlets were used by the infantry in training; they were uncomfortable and impossibly cumbersome, and their practical value in the event of all - out gas warfare is doubtful. The respirator was redesigned in 1936, the face piece and hose having a khaki fabric covering over the black rubber beneath. The hose connects to a filter within a red - painted ribbed metal box inside the haversack; brass vents in the haversack base allowed air circulation through the filter and along the hose to the mask; exhaled air was expelled through a non - return valve in the round metal muzzle of the face piece.

(Below) Later service respirator as produced from 1941 with bare rubber face piece and hose. The Mk VII haversack has a non - removable sling, and a round metal reel on the left side - when worn at the alert the haversack securing cord is passed round the body and fastened by winding it around this. Some of the haversack contents include anti-dim kits, packs of Mk II and Mk III eyeshields, cotton waste, and a tin of anti - gas ointment No 2 containing ten tubes. As the war progressed improved ointments appeared: No 3 (grey - painted tin) and No 5 (blue - painted tin).
Left of the haversack is the Wallet, Anti - Gas; made from the same fabric as anti - gas clothing, it was intended to protect the paybook and other personal papers from contamination.

Cavalry Pattern Greatcoat

Winter 1940/41, and a trooper of the Royal Armoured Corps steps out wearing a cavalry pattern greatcoat. This style, originating in 1917, was on issue to personnel of many corps at the beginning of the war. Many cavalrymen were drawn into the establishments of the fledgeling RAC; and the Royal Tank Regiment also wore the cavalry pattern greatcoat. This is double-breasted, with a plain unbelted back; the collar of this garment was deeper than that of the infantry 1939 or 1940 pattern greatcoats (this is well defined in the detail photograph); and the flaps of the two side pockets were mounted straight rather than angled. Though not apparent in this image the overall length was shorter than the infantry equivalent. Internally its front and back were almost fully lined in white wool fabric.

Our trooper sports on his black beret the early RAC cap badge which predated the mailed fist design of 1941. On his coat epaulettes brass titles are still in evidence.

Early Denim Overalls

(Left) Summer 1941, and an unfortunate private soldier is seen at the cookhouse door, wearing for fatigues the denim battledress which was, as already mentioned, the direct predecessor of the Battledress, Serge. His blouse and trousers are of the early pattern, but the trousers have the modified field dressing pocket with double pleat and button fastening introduced into manufacture in mid - 1940. By the outbreak of war the blouse had been modified so that the front, pocket and cuff buttons were exposed. These buttons were of plastic with looped metal shanks which passed through holes in the cloth and were secured by brass or grey metal split rings inside. Blouses in the early war period tended to have flat buttons; later buttons became dished. The trousers were also amended, losing the original right hand rear pocket. Our private's suit is of a particularly brown hue, typical of early denim battledress. At least three shades of denim fabric appear to have been used; and one example has been noted as having a shade number specified on its size label.

(Right & far right) Rear and side details of early Trousers, Overall, Denim in a green shade of fabric. Note the uneven placing of the belt loops, as on the serge battledress; this is explained by the presence on the early battledress uniforms - both denim and serge - of a right hand rear pocket which made it impracticable to fit a belt loop above it. Note also the size label, an early example in reinforced paper rather than white cotton fabric; it was also attached in the corresponding position on battledress trousers. The early field dressing pocket has one pleat and no button. Rather than wearing braces this man supports his trousers with a 1903 pattern leather belt, still in use with several corps in 1940 (and sometimes seen adorned with souvenir cap badges and brass insignia, as had been fashionable in the Great War). Hanging from a lanyard around his waist is his clasp knife, with checkered black bakelite grips; it is the larger prewar type common at this period, complete with a marlin spike. A known variant has a blade, tin opener (pointed design) and bone handle.

"Spud bashing" - not only a regular cookhouse fatigue, but also the sergeant major's favourite method of dealing with minor defaulters; potato peeling was an alternative to being put on CO's orders, with the risk of more serious punishment. The "dixie" at his feet was a universal item used for preparing food at all levels, in the front line as well as in barracks, since before World War I. The denims' resemblance to serge battledress included the buttoning ankle tabs, and the placing of the label on the inside blouse pocket.

Ablutions

(Right) The facilities available to the ordinary soldier for performing his ablutions were neither modern nor luxurious. Here a sapper of the Royal Engineers makes the best of things in accommodation which would have been familiar to his grandfather. With his washing kit in his "holdall" by his side, he digests some of last year's news before putting it to better use in these times of chronic paper shortage. He has risen early to prepare for morning parade, protected against the dank chill of washhouse and latrine by his Vest, Short Sleeved, Wool and Drawers, Woollen, Long, his battledress trousers and service pullover. The khaki pullover has a V - neck, knitted cuffs and waistband; loose and long on the body, not fitted, it was issued in a numbered range of sizes and when worn under BD it was tucked into the trousers. It remained the same pattern throughout the war, though pullovers were sometimes adapted by officers to allow shirt epaulettes to be worn through the shoulders to display rank.

(Below) The white cotton wash roll or holdall, with typical contents - from left to right: Spare boot laces, specified as being carried in the holdall; bone comb; toothbrush (this example with plastic handle, earlier models had bone); shaving brush with wooden handle (some variants have a white metal collar; late war examples are brown bakelite); safety razor (brown bakelite type, dated examples before 1943 not known; earlier razors were commercial, or aluminium WD issue); issue knife, fork and spoon stamped with soldier's number. Soap, tooth powder or paste and razor blades were usually of commercial brands bought by the soldier when needed; these could be tucked into the pocket at the left end of the roll, and shaving soap sticks into one of the spare loops. These items are laid out in kit inspection style, when the button stick would also be placed in the holdall.

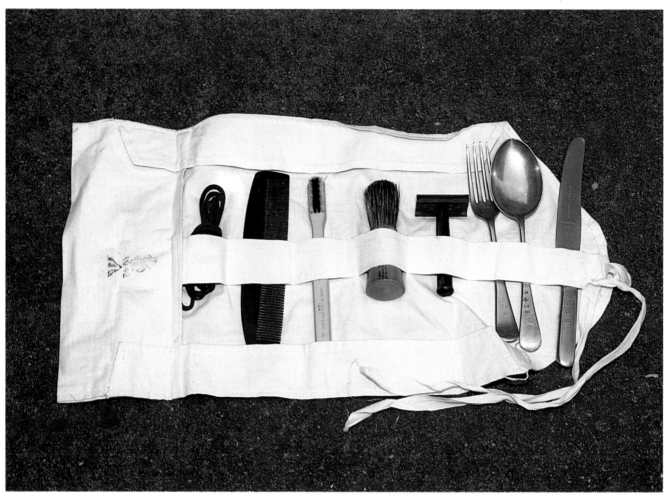

(Left) The soldier to the left of this pair wears the other ranks' issue Shirt, Wool Angora, Collarless. In use by all troops until the last year of the war (when the Shirt, Collar Attached was introduced), it pulls on over the head and is fastened with three buttons, at first gunmetal and later plastic. The neck band is of khaki drill fabric, and is not designed to take a separate collar. (However, that is not to say that ingenious soldiers did not add collars from spare shirt tail fabric, for wear with a tie when walking out - a distinctly unofficial fashion seen from the middle years of the war.)

This sapper supports his early pattern trousers (identifiable by their belt loops) with a 1903 pattern leather belt. Apart from a few examples of braces with an additional piece of striped elastic fabric making a Y-shape at the rear, most issue braces had the disadvantage of being inflexible and prone to strain, thus pulling off the buttons - particularly the brass buttons on early BD trousers. Whenever practical, working soldiers allowed the braces to dangle so as to avoid this. An old soldier's trick was to substitute "bachelor" buttons - metal buttons pushed through the fabric and fitted like a rivet - to avoid the constant chore of replacing braces buttons.

(Right) With white service towel slung over his arm, our sapper displays the rear pocket detail of early pattern BD trousers. Although exposed buttonholes are a feature of the later 1940 pattern BD, at least one pair of early pattern trousers with an exposed rear pocket button is known. Another item issued with the 1903 belt is this leather loop with a brass spring clip for suspending the clasp knife. The knife illustrated is a commonly seen smaller pattern, with checkered bakelite grips, a blade and a tin opener. Naturally, many different commercial patterns were also privately acquired by soldiers.

(Bottom right) 1940 pattern BD trousers; note the size label, and the position of the buttons to which the rear waistband of the blouse was attached. The white cotton service braces had leather buttonhole tabs and gunmetal fittings, including two types of adjusting front buckles; the earlier relied on the tension of the braces strap to hold it in place, the later had a pivoting toothed bar to grip it.

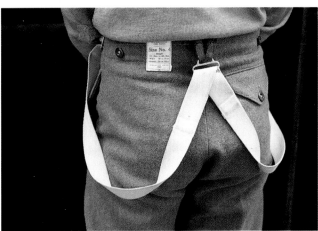

Cyclist, 1941

(Left & below) Spring 1941: still officially on the alert for German invasion, some infantry units are operating as cycle - mounted "rapid reaction forces". Here a cyclist arrives at a checkpoint, his kit covered against rain by the brown and green camouflaged ground sheet/cape. His progress is checked by a teenage Home Guard who has yet to reach the age of enlistment. Battledress is still in too short supply for issue to the Home Guard, and he wears a motley suit of denim issued as a stop - gap. As yet no complete set of equipment has been devised for Britain's part time army; the lad only has a 1903 leather belt to support the bayonet of his US - donated P17 rifle (the red band a reminder that this .30in weapon does not take standard .303in ammunition).

The cyclist's camouflaged ground sheet/cape is of the same design as the plain brown model manufactured until 1941, but with added swathes of green colour in a cloud pattern rather similar to that used on contemporary Army vehicles and RAF aircraft; this particular example dates from 1940.

(Right) The cyclist wears the long 1907 bayonet of his SMLE rifle not dangling from his left hip, but with its frog looped over the pack attachment strap and its scabbard tucked under the lower pack strap to restrict movement. While obviously particularly convenient for cyclists, this practice was by no means unique to them. He takes off his ground sheet cape to get at his BD blouse pocket. Note the anti - gas cape neatly rolled ready for use on the shoulders, resting on top of the small pack and secured to the body by two white tapes.

(Left) This head and shoulders detail shows the unlined collar of the early pattern BD blouse worn over the collarless shirt. Note also the method of attaching the anti - gas cape in its (theoretically) quick release position behind the shoulders. The two white tapes emerging from the roll support the cape. They pass forward over the shoulders; down and through the retaining string or D - ring on the side of the respirator haversack (a Mk IV is shown here); then back around the body to be tied off below the pack. The cord emerges, like the tapes, from inside the rolled cape; it passes forward and is tied to the upper ring of the respirator haversack, easy to hand. In the event of a gas alert the soldier quickly unties the cord and gives it a sharp tug; this releases the cape so that it unrolls down his back, supported by the white tapes at the shoulders, and can be shrugged on quickly over his equipment.

(Below) A neatly blancoed example of the 37 pattern Anklet, Web, with the earlier webbing straps which were later replaced by leather for a better grip in the open - frame brass buckles. The BD trousers were supposed to bag down one inch over the top; for smartness soldiers sometimes put weights around the inside of this "pull - down". The ammunition boots were issued dull black with a dimple finish all over. For field use they were treated only with waterproof (and gasproof) dubbin, but soldiers invariably kept a "best" pair for parade and walking out. Like the boot illustrated, these had the toecaps smoothed (a painstaking process involving a hot spoon and a piece of bone) and then polished to a mirror finish.

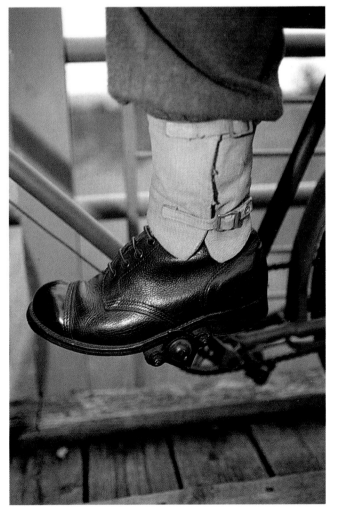

(Above) The private produces from his breast pocket his AB (Army Book) 64 Pt I, the Soldier's Service and Pay Book, as proof of his identity to this wary young sentry. The pay book came in two sections, Parts I and II. Part I was issued on enlistment, and contained particulars of service entered at company level, as well as a will form; it was to be carried at all times as a form of identification. Part II (see page 71) was only issued when proceeding on active service.

Coloured Field Service Caps & Helmet Flashes

The field service cap, whose origins can be traced back to the 19th century, was reintroduced to most units of the British Army in 1937. Each regiment and corps had its own distinctive colours, the coloured sections being divided into the crown, body, peak, and curtain, in some cases with additional coloured piping to the crown, peak and/or curtain. The coloured FS cap was, in most instances, an optional and privately purchased item worn when off duty with SD or blues, its use later being extended to wear with BD. Quality varied greatly depending on cash outlay; the cheapest types were quite rough, but if they could afford them other ranks were able to buy officers' quality caps of the finest doeskin fabric with velvet sweatbands. Officers' versions followed the same basic colourings as ORs' but were frequently adorned with additional piping and gilt buttons.

(Above) At left, a private of the Royal Army Medical Corps wears the coloured FS of his corps, with a dull cherry red crown and body and dark blue peak and curtain; the officers' version had gold piping to the crown, peak and curtain. The coloured FS cap of The Devonshire Regiment, worn by the soldier at right, has a black peak and curtain with dark green body and crown, the crown being piped in red. The same colour scheme was used by officers of the Devonshires.

(Right) The 11th Hussars (Prince Albert's Own) had a very distinctive item of headdress dating back to the late 1920s when the hussars converted from horses to armoured cars. The issue SD cap being deemed unsuitable attire in such confined vehicles, this brown and crimson beret was adopted. It was so distinctive that no badge was worn with it.

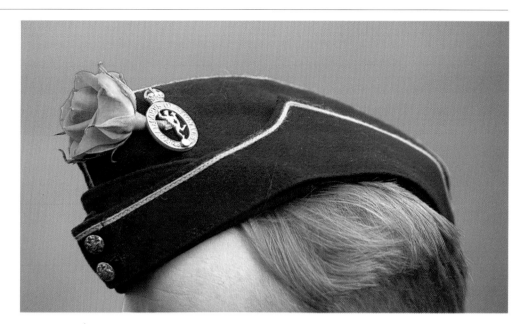

(Right) On national saints' days it was common practice for units to wear their national flower tucked behind the cap badge - a rose on St.George's Day, a thistle for St.Andrew, a leek for St.David and a shamrock for St.Patrick. Individual regiments might also commemorate particularly significant dates in their history, such as the "Minden roses" worn on 1 August by the descendants of the six infantry regiments which won that battle honour in 1759 (e.g. Suffolk Regiment, Royal Hampshires, Royal Welch Fusiliers, etc.). A poppy was worn by all units on Armistice Day, 11 November. This signaller from the Royal Corps of Signals celebrates 23 April (St.George's Day) with a red English rose. The Signals' coloured FS cap had a dark blue body, peak and curtain, with a light blue crown and light blue piping to the crown and curtain.

(Centre right) Officer's quality FS cap of The East Yorkshire Regiment: dark red crown piped white, dark red body, black peak and curtain. The linings are usually in silk or rayon material with the makers' or retailers' stamped details or labels. Officers of the East Yorkshires wore a collar badge on this type of headdress, a practice later carried over to the GS cap, where it had a square black backing. The regimental buttons on the front of the curtain are of the officers' embossed type worn on mess kit - with which this cap was worn before the war.

(Bottom right) Before the war it had been a common practice to mark steel helmets with regimental or corps badges and devices; these were normally transferred or painted badges applied to the front or coloured unit flashes applied to the left side. A number of BEF units sported such markings in 1940, but as the war progressed they became much less common (with the obvious exception of authorised identification marks such as those displayed by Military Police). This black and green triangular flash worn on the left side of the helmet by a soldier of the Devonshires echoes the colours of their FS cap.

Tank Crew Overalls, 1942

The short lived black two-piece suit of the prewar RTC was gradually replaced by BD serge and denims following their introduction in 1939. However, the "universal" new uniform was not quite as adaptable as had been hoped, and the RTR, among others, were soon looking for a uniform more suited to their specific requirements. The tank crew overalls introduced in 1942 were the first real attempt at providing clothing designed after careful consideration of its intended use.

(Right) The tanker's overalls were made from an unlined heavy cotton fabric with a water-repellent finish, fastened up the front by buttons concealed by a fly flap. It had no chest pockets, but an open top pocket closed by a press stud was positioned above the front of each hip; and like the BD, the overalls had a flap-top map pocket on the left thigh and a dressing pocket on the right hip. A shaped, flap-top pocket at the right upper thigh allowed for the carriage of a revolver. Wrist and ankle closures were adjustable by buttoned tabs. Zippered vents at each hip allowed access to clothing worn beneath. Here, the overalls are worn by a crewman from the 17th/21st Lancers.

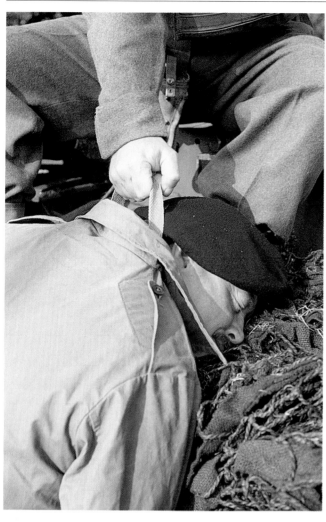

(Left) A webbing harness was stitched inside the front face of the suit, passing down and back under the crotch and finishing behind the wearer's neck in a short, strong "grab handle". This well thought out addition was to make it easier to pull a wounded crewman from the awkward confines and small hatches of an AFV - a difficult and harrowing task at any time. For some reason this harness was not included in later designs of overalls.

(Left below) The side vent zip, field dressing pocket, and special revolver pocket. This latter reduced the risk of snagging previously associated with separate web belts and holsters; but it proved to be uncomfortable and much less adaptable than a belt and holster, and this feature too was omitted from subsequent designs.

(Below) Interior detail of the harness arrangement as it runs up the chest, the grab handle and shoulder reinforcement pads, and the typed label on the right inner face of the eight - button fly front fastening.

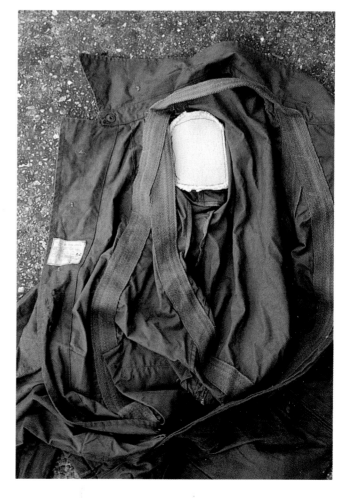

Field Service Marching Order, 1941

December 1941: a Royal Artillery gunner, having endured a long and uncomfortable overnight rail journey, arrives at last at his own front door. When his brief leave is over he will move on with his unit to a new posting; and since he is "changing station" he carries his whole world with him, packed into his web equipment and kit bag. The webbing complete with large pack was termed Field Service Marching Order. During the early war period, under the threat of invasion, men on leave for more than 48 hours took their rifles home with them (though without ammunition); this is the sturdy and accurate bolt - action Short Magazine Lee Enfield Rifle No 1 Mk III, the standard personal weapon since before the Great War, which took ten .303in rounds in the removable magazine.

The kit bag in white canvas would have the soldier's name, rank and regimental number stencilled on it in black. In the early part of the war dark blue kit bags were also used. Kit bags were closed either with a knotted draw cord or a privately acquired padlock and shackle. From 1944 there also appeared some tan kitbags with a side carrying handle and a shoulder sling, a spring clip fastening this to a metal shackle through brass eyelets around the mouth of the bag.

(Right) The gunner wears the red and blue coloured FS cap of the Royal Artillery; and his arm of service is also identified by the strip of red and blue cloth, 2ins x ¼in, sewn to both upper sleeves. These were introduced in September 1940 for wear on battledress blouses and greatcoats by all ranks and branches of service, in appropriate colour combinations. On his belt note the 37 pattern double cartridge carriers, issued to corps other than infantry who had no need to carry Bren magazines or large amounts of rifle ammunition. This distinction was phased out from 1943.

(Left) FSMO accomodated all the items required in the field, including the greatcoat (which was folded into the large pack when not worn). The large pack was the unchanged 08 pattern; its attachments - strap ends and buckles - were compatible with the 37 pattern L - shaped pack straps. The pack was left behind in unit transport when the soldier went into "battle order". Apart from the greatcoat it officially accomodated his washing kit, towel, sewing and darning kit in a "housewife" pouch, the knitted cap comforter, soft uniform cap, and perhaps plimsolls; in marching order the helmet was secured to it by the crossed support straps, and the respirator was slung either so that it sat above or below the pack or - as here - in the alert position. In FMSO the haversack was buckled to the brace ends on his left hip, over the bayonet. The kit bag carried spare uniform and other clothing: his best battledress, spare boots, shirts and underwear.

Although it is hidden here by his equipment, this soldier wears the 1940 pattern greatcoat which was by now replacing the 1939 pattern. An expansion pleat was added, running down from the upper back; this allowed web equipment or extra layers of clothing to be worn more easily under the greatcoat. The rear half - belt with three button adjustment was retained.

Coat 1A

As part of the Army's scheme of wet weather clothing, the MP pictured here is wearing the rubberised khaki cotton Coat 1A. This garment was issued to those whose duties periodically required them to be out of doors in all weathers - e.g. the Corps of Military Police, fulfilling their roles as security sentries, foot patrols and directors of traffic. The coat is of simple construction, being single-breasted with a fly front and two concealed front pockets with deep flaps. Our Redcap, with his respirator and helmet slung on his left hip, returns to barracks after coming off duty - he has taken off his MP brassard, in the same way that a civil policeman of the period took off his blue and white striped duty band.

(Left) Mk II helmet with Military Police markings, worn slung on the respirator haversack - common practice for all service personnel when respirators and helmets were to be carried at all times. The red band painted round the helmet denotes the Provost Wing of the CMP. These helmet bands followed the different SD cap covers worn by MPs: white indicated traffic personnel, and blue MPs providing security for vital points.

ORs' Utility Service Dress

(Left) Early winter 1942: in the aftermath of a Luftwaffe raid a Gefreiter from a downed bomber crew has been picked up by the civil authorities, and is being handed over from the custody of the local police to that of the CMP for escort on the journey which will eventually lead to a POW camp.

Throughout the war certain other ranks retained service dress; the most notable were the CMP, who continued to wear SD while not serving in combat areas. This corporal (all MPs had NCO rank) is dressed for sentry duty or foot patrol. His red cap cover and brassard make him readily identifiable. His tunic is of the utility pattern introduced as an economy measure from 1942, without pocket pleats. It also resembles the modified battledress in that from mid - 1940 the service dress tunic had a fabric lining added to the collar interior.

(Right) He wears the leather 1903 pattern belt with open holster, ammunition pouch and cross strap assembly prescribed for this order of dress. Holster and pouch were originally part of pistol order with 1908 or 1914 pattern equipment, but were now produced to fit the 1903 belt. The cross strap fixes through a brass fitting at the back of the holster, and at the rear to the same fitting mounted on a leather loop slid onto the belt. The Redcap wears the lanyard of his .38 revolver around the shoulder rather than the neck - this was doubtless felt safer for duties which might involve physical altercations with his "customers".

Physical Training

Spring 1944: after a warm - up run round the camp perimeter during their six weeks' basic training, raw young recruits - who will fill the depleted ranks of the infantry as replacements before the war is over - wait to be put through their paces by a corporal Physical Training Instructor.

The PTI's early pattern battledress sports a sleeve array characteristic of the period; the dull anonymity of 1940 has gone forever.

From its inception in September 1940 the Army Physical Training Corps shared with the Foot Guards the official distinction of wearing coloured cloth shoulder titles rather than black on khaki slip - ons; these are printed in red on black, the Corps' distinctive colours. Below the title was worn the insignia of the formation – regional command, army, corps, division or brigade; in this case it is the apple of Northern Command, where this training depot is located. Below the organisation patch is the field service strip in APTC colours - black, red, black; these strips might be of felt on a fabric or paper backing, or embroidered onto khaki cloth. The crossed swords badge above his rank chevrons on both sleeves identifies him as a PTI.

(Below) Practising the fireman's lift - which one day they may have reason to use in the front line. Woollen and cotton vests or singlets were sometimes worn for PT; cotton PT shorts were normally dark blue, with a drawstring or elasticated waist, but occasionally khaki drill.

(Right) A cotton aertex PT vest manufactured by Bukta Sportswear. This pullover vest has a round collar and cloth-covered buttons on the front placket. A variant exists in a cream flannel fabric.

(Below right) Brown canvas and rubber PT shoes - a mundane part of every soldier's kit, worn in camp when off duty or on campaign when out of the line. These plimsolls were also used on occasion instead of boots by infantry patrols, and even during Commando raids, when silent movement was vital.

(Left) The smock worn by the trainee is part of a two-piece suit in green denim fabric which appeared in 1941; the design was later retained for all subsequent mountain and arctic smocks. (This example is curiously labelled as a Smock, Snow; apparently contradictory labels are quite often found in various smocks of wartime manufacture.) It is of pullover design with two pleated breast pockets, two concealed skirt pockets with deep flaps, and broad white drawtapes at the hood and lower hem.

(Below) Rear of twill mountain breeches, with the same belt loop arrangement as early battledress, and two flapped pockets.

(Opposite) The failed Norwegian expedition of 1940 had highlighted the Army's unpreparedness to fight in snow-covered or mountainous terrain. After an initial trial training a Guards battalion in ski-marching at the beginning of 1940 a more serious attempt saw the conversion of an entire Scottish division - 52nd (Lowland) - to the mountain warfare role. Procurement of a new range of clothing and equipment started in 1940, and training in Scotland began in 1941. Here a trainee (left) and his Free Norwegian instructor both wear ski caps and khaki twill Breeches, Mountaineering - note strap and button fastening below the knee. The trainee wears long Socks, Heavy Wool, Knit and short puttees, with cleated mountain boots; the instructor, long puttees and ammunition boots.

(Left) The mountain boots have a Continental appearance, being copied - like most of this kit - from prewar civilian styles. They have reinforced toes, a leather loop at the rear to retain long laces passed around the ankle, and steel cleats; further heavy cleats were fixed to the sole and star-shaped studs to the heel. Not illustrated are the Army arctic boots "Finnish pattern", an early design sometimes retro-fitted with US Army cleats for use as mountain boots. In brown reversed leather treated so that it would remain supple in extreme cold, these had bulbous toecaps to accomodate extra socks, and shaped heels allowing use with skis.

(Left) Copying the design of the green denim Smock and Trousers, Snow, this tan windproof smock appeared in 1942. Made in lightweight cotton fabric with brown plastic battledress - type buttons, it has a narrow white cotton drawtape round the hood and a thicker tape in the hem. The tan windproof suit exists in two subtly different shades: one plain and pale in colour, the other - illustrated here - slightly browner and more mottled in appearance. The Smock, Snow, Camouflaged, Heavy Weight appeared in the same year.

(Opposite) Precariously traversing a ledge, the Norwegian instructor wears his fully laden "Bergen" rucksack. These came in tan or, later, in green duck canvas; an early webbing example is also known. The bag has one rear and two side external pockets, two straps on the base and one on each side for attaching extra stowage, and long straps on the entry flap to accomodate bulky or protruding items. External stowage includes snow shoes, an ice axe, and, at the bottom, an arctic bedroll in its carrying bag. Early examples of the Bergen sometimes have the edges of the entry flap and pocket flaps trimmed with leather or puttee tape. It should be borne in mind that Army Commandos, who also trained extensively in hostile Scottish terrain, made use of such items from the mountain cadres' equipment as mountain boots, windproof smocks, Jumpers Heavy Weight and Bergens.

(Right) Front face of a Bergen showing metal supporting frame, fixing straps and web carrying straps. The main body of the rucksack is fixed to a rigid metal supporting frame by leather tabs at the base, and leather straps through a leather cover around the shoulder. Note also the arctic bedroll bag, issue wood and rope snow shoes, and long-shafted ice axe.

(Above & above right) The ski cap appeared in 1943, made from the same fabric as the FS cap, though proofed to be water-resistant. The lining of wool shirt fabric was only partly fixed by hooks and eyes, which when detached allowed earflaps and a partial neck flap to be stowed underneath it. The earflaps could be secured under the chin with a length of puttee tape, or tied up over the crown; some known examples with sheepskin stitched to the inside are probably postwar civilian modifications. Note (above) the national insignia worn by this Free Norwegian officer serving with the British Army - British troops sometimes added their cap badges. The underside of the long visor was lined with black fabric to cut down snow glare. The sweater worn by the soldier (above right) is non-regulation, knitted by a relative or a charity "comforts" organisation.

(Centre right) A brew-up, using a Primus type stove to melt snow in the mess tin to make tea; such commercial stoves were often purchased for use by such units. A tin of soup is set ready in the foreground; such ration items were sometimes finished in green paint, but often in bright gold or brass, with black stencilled description and instructions; these were familiar in the 14-man/day "compo" ration boxes issued from 1943. An ingenious and popular item issued from 1944 was the self-heating soup tin; this had a central heating wick in a tube, which the soldier lit after removing a coin-sized rubber-sealed plug in the top.

(Bottom right) The military thermos flask, its metal covering in black stippled paint finish; these have makers' details and year of manufacture embossed into the base. A supplementary three-piece felt cover was also produced, to give shock protection and to insulate the flask for longer periods.

Buttons

Main patterns of uniform buttons. The measurements quoted are a guide - variations will be found. Large size buttons were used on greatcoats and service dress tunics; the officer's pattern were of better quality and their greatcoat buttons slightly larger than the ORs' equivalent. The small size button was for pocket flaps and epaulettes, and was also used as a front button on dress blues and KD tunics. The gorget - size button was also used on the SD and FS caps. All types were available in regimental and corps patterns as well as the General Service pattern bearing the Royal arms. Regimental variations did exist, such as the black composition buttons worn by the Rifle regiments.

Column 1, top to bottom: *Officer's greatcoat button, "large" (26mm), Royal Signals; other ranks' service dress button, "large" (23.5mm), GS pattern; other ranks' SD button, "small" (17mm); cap & gorget button (12mm).*

Column 2: *Economy buttons in "vegetable ivory" i.e. plastic: "large" (24mm); "small" (18mm); colours varied from green through to red - brown. These were used on greatcoats and SD (particularly ATS SD).*

Column 3: *Battledress buttons: early two - piece brass (16mm); stamped brass (17.5mm); economy stamped grey metal (17.5mm); economy vegetable ivory (17.5mm). The sharp edges of the stamped buttons were notorious for cutting through the retaining stitches, leading to loss.*

Column 4: *Early and later patterns of revolving shank button (19mm), vegetable ivory - used on denims and on later pattern BD dressing pockets and epaulettes; grey metal button (14mm) for ORs' collarless shirt; vegetable ivory shirt button (15mm) for ORs' late pattern collar - attached shirt.*

(Left) A novelty: an escape compass concealed in a large size GS uniform button made in two pieces with a screw thread - it is unlikely that this would be discovered during any routine search following capture. This example also contains a miniature photograph of a loved one.

Scottish Officer's Service Dress

(Opposite) Autumn 1943: England is an armed camp, and London has a distinctly cosmopolitan air as the armies of the free world prepare for their return to occupied Western Europe. A lieutenant of the Gordon Highlanders chats with a lieutenant of Free Polish paratroopers. For walking out the Gordon's order of the day is service dress. Officers of both Highland and Lowland Scottish regiments wore a wool gabardine SD tunic with rounded cutaway skirt fronts, like those of Scottish other ranks, and with the false cuff swept up towards the rear seam. This "doublet" tunic is worn with appropriate regimental brass buttons and bronze collar insignia. He wears the Glengarry of the regiment with officers' pattern badge; Gordon tartan trews (Government sett with a yellow overstripe); black laced shoes; and a Sam Browne belt. During the war officers newly commissioned into Highland regiments were discouraged from purchasing kilts, considered an extravagant use of resources; during the war years they were seldom worn, and never in the field except by some pipers.

(Above) "Hey, mac, can you tell me the way to Lie - sester Square?" Hailed by a USAAF staff sergeant, our Polish and Scottish subalterns puzzle over a US Army broadsheet about options for entertainment and interest while on furlough which the airman produces from his overnight holdall. Note the Gordon's red toori, massive officer-quality Glengarry badge, and bronze Egyptian sphinx "collar dogs" recalling a battle honour of the old 92nd Foot.

(Above) Officers of Allied contingents from occupied countries who continued the struggle from Britain after 1940 soon acquired British Army uniforms embellished with their national insignia; and this lieutenant of the 1st Polish Parachute Brigade may stand as a representative example. He has an early war service dress fitted with Polish buttons, and he wears (unlike British officers) a cloth shoulder title on the SD tunic - POLAND in white on red. The light grey beret with the Polish national badge, and the officers' pattern yellow - piped grey collar patches with parachute insignia, identify his arm of service. His Polish parachutist's qualification brevet is pinned to the left breast, and pairs of silver rank stars to his epaulettes.

Windproof Smock

(Opposite) Italy, spring 1944: an infantry patrol wearing two - piece windproof suits and the skeleton assault jerkin. The windproofs, made from a tightly woven fabric, were worn over the wool serge battle-dress. The pullover style Smock, Drab, had two breast and two skirt pockets fastened with buttoned flaps; it had a full hood with tightening drawtape, and a second drawtape around the lower hem, but the sleeve cuffs were a weak point - there was no means of tightening them around the wrist. The trousers had a draw-tape waist with no fly; the knees had reinforcing patches, and a map pocket was placed on the left thigh. Fabric weight and colour varied depending on the manufacturer.

(Left & below) The skeleton assault jerkin (a simplified version of the load - carrying assault jerkin illus-trated on pages 82 - 83) saw limited use in Italy and by Commandos in NW Europe. A simple yoke of water-proof brown canvas, its two front pockets allowed the carriage of up to six Bren magazines or ten grenades, although the toggle and loop fasten-ing was inadequate and allowed grenades and other items to slip out when on the move. The jerkin origi-nally came in a range of sizes; this wasteful approach was eventually abandoned in favour of laced side sections allowing one size to be adjusted to fit all wearers; it is believed that this modification never saw issue during the war. A small loop at the left waist allowed the carriage of a spike bay-onet and scabbard, but there was no provision for the attachment of additional kit. However, the plain back of the yoke did enable the use of a pack or rucksack.

(Above) Boots, Ski, March - a dual purpose walking boot which dou-bled as a ski boot. Note the slightly squared toe and the grooved heel which fitted the bindings of the mil-itary cross - country skis.

US War Aid Clothing

(Left) *Italy, 1944: an infantryman wearing US - made battledress. This was one of the anomalies of wartime procurement: while trans - Atlantic shipping space was at such a premium that many items of US web equipment were manufactured in the UK, at the same time US factories were producing BD and other equipment for the British Army. Production of BD began in January 1943 from specifications drawn up in autumn 1942; its issue was limited to Italy and the Mediterranean theatre. Battledress, Olive Drab, War Aid was of noticeably better fabric and a greener shade than British production. The most noticeable identifying feature is the fly front on the blouse but with exposed buttons to the unpleated pockets. Blouses had two labels on the internal right pocket, one unmistakably American giving contract and stock numbers, and the other giving typically British size ranges.*

(Right) *Stevens Savage of Chicopee Falls, Massachusetts, produced well over a million No 4 rifles and spike bayonets. Both were marked with the company's boxed S device, and the rifle action was stamped "US Property"; the rifle is also recognisable by slight differences around the bolt head. The Canadian Longbranch factory also produced vast numbers of No 4 rifles and bayonets for British use.*

(Right) Greatcoat, OD, WA. This was identical to the 1940 pattern in that it had an expanding pleat to the back; in all other respects both types resembled the 1939 pattern greatcoat. As with the BD the fabric was of a finer quality and had a greener hue than British - made coats; the shoulder area lining fabric was similar to that used in the US olive drab field jacket. In the field the brass GS buttons were allowed to dull naturally to prevent reflections, or painted. This lance - corporal of infantry behind the line wears a cap comforter.

(Left) Both the SMLE and No 4 rifles were loaded using five - round charger clips, issued in 50 - round cotton bandoliers which could be folded into the basic pouches or worn slung. The ten - round magazines were removable, but the standard method of loading was to engage the clip in guides above the receiver, push the rounds down out of it with the thumb, and discard the clip; closing the bolt chambered the top round and cocked the rifle.

In addition to War Aid battledress uniforms, American - made khaki drill clothing was also to be seen in the Italian theatre. Much KD clothing in use in Italy had been brought across from North Africa with the advancing 8th Army. This Jacket, Bush, WA is easily identifiable from its British counterpart, being made from the same herringbone twill as used for US Army fatigue and anti - gas protective clothing, while the British KD was made from heavy drill fabric of an even weave. American manufacturers also produced WA shorts and trousers in a tropical khaki colour, but these items were made from a heavy cotton rather than HBT.

The poor quality web equipment at this Irish Guardsman's side is of Indian manufacture. Much equipment made in India found its way to troops in North Africa and Italy, where the 8th Army included very large numbers of Indian Army units. Indian web was of a noticeably lighter construction and used thinner gauge brass for its fittings.

Officers' US War Aid Clothing

(Right) British officers in Italy wearing US War Aid BD blouses, with (at left) Indian - made trousers, and (at right) WA trousers - note the contrasting shades of khaki. The captain in the khaki FS cap wears The King's Shropshire Light Infantry's K.S.L.I. shoulder title above the white triangle patch of the 1st Infantry Division. His companion wearing a SD cap is a major of the Army Dental Corps, attached to the headquarters of General Mark Clarke's US 5th Army; he wears the 5th Army patch on both sleeves of his BD blouse in the British manner - his American counterparts wore shoulder sleeve insignia on the left only.

(Left) Detail of cuff, waistband and field dressing pocket of the WA battledress. The different buttons used on the blouse and trousers are quite evident, both being typically American military patterns. The dressing pocket is distinctive in that it retains the single pleat of early British type but with an added button. The buckle is typically British, but on some WA BD the US enlisted man's frame belt buckle was used as a fastening.

(Right) The unpleated breast pocket of the WA BD blouse, with visible button. The lining of the officer's pressed-open collar has been scrubbed, which often reduced the fabric to an off-white shade. Worn above the pocket are the ribbons of the 1939-1943 Star (later 1939-1945) and the Italy Star. By the middle war years the former was starting to be displayed; it was awarded to all ranks of all the armed services, in the case of the Army for six months' service in an operational overseas command - the time qualification was waived for casualties and certain other categories. The Italy Star was awarded for operational service throughout the Mediterranean theatre other than the North African mainland.

(Below) Sweaters, WA, were manufactured in light milk chocolate coloured wool as used for the US Army issue five-button Sweater, High Neck; they otherwise resembled the standard issue British pullover. This officer is wearing Indian -

manufactured BD trousers - in comparison with the War Aid clothing the overall quality was inferior and the fabric was quite rough. The two label system used in WA clothing can be seen on the internal pocket of the BD blouse. It should be noted that some labels used "OD, WA" in the description while others deleted the "OD".

(Below right) American issue shirts, both enlisted men's and officers' patterns, were used extensively by British troops in Italy; this major wears one of the many slightly differing styles of American officers' shirts. They had attached collars and epaulettes as standard, unlike most British shirts with their awkward detachable collars. Other ranks adapted EMs' shirts by adding shoulder loops to take buttoned - on epaulettes; divisional insignia were then worn on khaki slip - ons.
The waistband of WA BD trousers was darted to allow for a better fit, and these darts are visible here above the field dressing pocket.

Officer's Mackintosh & Raincoat; Officer's GS Cap

(Left) Pursuing a policy instigated in 1943 the Army Quartermaster's Clothing Department created a range of uniform items for use by officers (and presumably senior NCOs); these were made available for purchase as an alternative to those bought by officers from commercial retailers. Included in this range of garments were service dress caps, shirts and collars, braces, socks and suspenders, greatcoats, British warms, ankle and field boots and, as illustrated here, raincoats and mackintoshes.

The Raincoat, Officers, on the left is a classic trenchcoat design with belt and wrist straps, storm back and shoulders, removable epaulettes, leather "football" buttons and leather - covered buckles, and in this case a tartan lining. This particular example, made in 1944, is worn by an officer in The East Yorkshire Regiment. He is in conversation on the steps to the mess with an officer of The Duke of Cornwall's Light Infantry who wears the rubberised cotton Mackintosh, Officers. This is single - breasted with plastic buttons, buttoning tabs at the cuffs and under the collar, an integral belt, two flapped internal pockets below the waist, and two internal adjustable straps to secure the skirts if required. It is unlined, and more utilitarian in appearance and quality, but has a detachable liner in beige wool which can be secured by buttons inside the coat.

(Right) Rear of mackintosh (left) and raincoat (right); note the latter's storm shoulders and the D - rings on the belt.

(Bottom right) Officer's quality General Service cap. The Cap, GS, was ordered into service to replace the khaki FS cap in most - but not all - regiments and corps from September 1943, but universal issue took some time. Officers were supposed to acquire caps when their men received them, some purchasing issue caps, others buying superior versions from commercial outfitters. This DCLI officer patronised the fashionable hatters Locke & Co.; his cap is made in khaki gabardine cloth, lined in the same fabric as the SD cap and with a leather sweatband. (Examples of gabardine khaki berets with a khaki fabric, as opposed to leather, headband were also manufactured for Locke & Co.) The tubular scarf is made of fine khaki wool; dated 1944, it is one of the items produced for sale through the QM stores.

Despatch Rider, 1944

(Left) May 1944: during the final build up to Operation Overlord a Don - R parks his BSA in a leafy Hampshire lane where he will deliver an urgent despatch to a traffic control headquarters. He wears the motorcyclist's outfit which began to enter service in 1942. Breeches or pantaloons and specially designed high protective boots replaced the BD trousers, anklets and ammunition boots. An adaptable one - piece proofed coat gave greater protection against rain and wind than the short jacket and leggings previously issued. A particular feature of the coat was the series of studs which allowed the skirt to be fastened around each leg, giving better protection when riding. The year 1942 also saw a move towards standardisation with the design of a rimless steel helmet shell for use by motorcyclists, armoured vehicle crews and Airborne troops. For motorcyclists it had a padded leather - covered interior and a leather neck and ear piece lined with soft fabric. This was fastened by a tongued roller buckle on the right of the chin, the end of the strap being fixed by a press stud. The rear of the leather harness was adjustable by means of a lace threaded through six eyelets; and, as on the pulp helmet, there were press - studded flaps over the ears.

(Right) The helmet worn here has a white painted band visible under the camouflage net, identifying a member of the traffic control branch of the Corps of Military Police. Note the details of the motorcyclist's boot, often worn with an extra pair of long socks. Later in the war a protective metal plate was added under the right instep to prevent excessive wear by the kick - start. The gauntlets remained unchanged throughout the war, typically in buff or brown leather; they were also used by some motor vehicle drivers and armoured crews.

Section III: Assault on Fortress Europe

The invasion of Normandy saw the first widespread use in action of two improved pieces of infantryman's equipment. The first was the Mk III helmet, designed to give greater all round protection, particularly across the back of the cranium and the neck. Manufactured from mid - 1943, the Mk III was worn by some of the assault troops on D - Day, and became more common as the liberation of North - West Europe progressed; however, it still had not entirely replaced the old Mk II by the end of the war in Europe. The second item was the light respirator, which also changed the profile of the Tommy by doing away with the bulky box respirator haversack on the chest, allowing greater freedom of movement.

As for the web equipment, the Mk II basic pouch, slightly lengthened to take the Sten gun magazines, had been in production since 1942 and was now in general use. The 08 pattern entrenching tool, with a carrier compatible with the 37 pattern equipment, had been re - introduced from the end of 1941. Its haft later acquired a metal fixture at the lower end to take the short spike bayonet of the No 4 rifle, for use as a probe for landmines; this adaption was not much seen until the end of 1944.

In 1944 the FS cap was beginning to be replaced by the more practical but horribly unstylish GS cap. Those categories which were excused this unpopular innovation - such as senior officers, and all ranks of the mechanised Motor Battalions within armoured formations - clung to their smarter khaki berets. The GS cap was in fact an isolated step back towards drabness. In the last year of the war the battledress uniform, even in the field, often displayed a riot of colourful insignia which echoed the experience of the Great War. When worn out of the front lines it reached its peak of official adornment and unofficial mod-

(Top) UK waters, 5 June 1944: men of a REME unit attached to 51st (Highland) Division have been officially informed - as if they needed telling - of the destination of the vast fleets assembled in the English Channel. Each has been issued "liberation" currency, and a handbook about France; note also (inset) the active service paybook, AB64 Pt II.

ification. Blouses already sported colourful shoulder titles, divisional patches, field service or brigade strips, often regimental or battalion flashes, shoulder lanyards, and campaign ribbons; the forearms became festooned with trade and skill - at - arms badges, good conduct and war service stripes. Even the GS cap was often brightened by coloured backings to the badges.

THE RIFLE GROUP

NUMBER 1 RIFLEMAN	NUMBER 2 RIFLEMAN	NUMBER 3 RIFLEMAN	CORPORAL SECTION COMMANDER	NUMBER 4 RIFLEMAN	NUMBER 5 RIFLEMAN	NUMBER 6 RIFLEMAN
SMLE RIFLE	SMLE RIFLE	SMLE RIFLE	STEN GUN Mk II	SMLE RIFLE	SMLE RIFLE	SMLE RIF
10 x RIFLE CHARGERS OF .303 AMMUNITION	10 x RIFLE CHARGERS OF .303 AMMUNITION	10 x RIFLE CHARGERS OF .303 AMMUNITION	160 x ROUNDS OF 9mm AMMUNITION	10 x RIFLE CHARGERS OF .303 AMMUNITION	10 x RIFLE CHARGERS OF .303 AMMUNITION	10 x RIF CHARGE OF .3C AMMUNIT
2 x MAGS FOR BREN GUN	2 x MAGS FOR BREN GUN	2 x MAGS FOR BREN GUN	5 MAGS FOR STEN	2 x MAGS FOR BREN GUN	2 x MAGS FOR BREN GUN	2 x M FOR B GU
1 x MILLS BOMB	1 x MILLS BOMB	1 x MILLS BOMB	2 x MILLS BOMBS	1 x MILLS BOMB	1 x MILLS BOMB	1 x MILLS BOMB
SHOVEL	SHOVEL	SHOVEL		PICK	SHOVEL	SHOVEL

The basic building block of the British infantry was the **section** led by a corporal. In 1939 this was eight men strong, all armed with rifles except for the LMG No 1 with the Bren gun; in mid - 1941 the section commander was officially listed as armed with a Thompson SMG; by 1944 he carried a Sten, and the section strength was up to ten men. One official scale of armament and equipment is shown in these diagrams; other sources vary in small details. For instance, in training pamphlets from 1942 onwards the section commander, rather than the Bren group commander, is listed as carrying a machete, together with wire cutters and a whistle, and a proportion of the grenades carried were to be No 77 smoke as well as No 36 fragmentation; in 1944 the riflemen were listed as carrying 100 rounds, rather than 50, of small arms ammunition. Note the issue of GS picks and shovels; these large tools were always necessary for digging slit trenches - the individual entrenching tool

was useless for getting two men right under cover quickly.

These lists all tend to be theoretical minimums; in actual combat the picture was always complicated by the need to carry as much ammunition as possible for the greedy support weapons, by casualties, personal choice, and other practicalities. When the average infantryman got out of his transport lorry and struck off on foot he would be loaded down with extra burdens, primarily of ammunition, grenades, radio batteries, etc. In battle his large pack, greatcoat and blankets would be left in the rear with the battalion transport. (It might be some time before a soldier was reunited with his large pack - if ever - so the wise campaigner kept his few but precious personal possessions in his haversack or his pockets at all times. The respirator case and even the entrenching tool pouch were also used for small kit.)

Three sections made up a **platoon**, with a command section consisting of the

THE BREN GROUP

LANCE CORPORAL BREN COMMANDER	NUMBER 1 BREN GUNNER	NUMBER 2 BREN GUNNER
SMLE No4 Mk1	FM BREN GUN	SMLE No4 Mk1
10 x RIFLE CHARGERS OF .303 AMMUNITION		10 x RIFLE CHARGERS OF .303 AMMUNITION
4 x MAGS FOR BREN GUN		5 x MAGS FOR BREN GUN
1 x MILLS BOMB	4 x MAGS FOR BREN GUN	1 x MILLS BOMB
MACHETE	BREN GUN TOOL WALLET	PICK / BREN SPARE PARTS ROLL

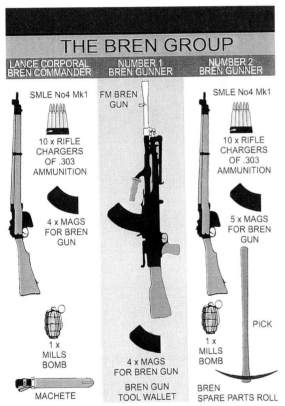

In battle individual circumstances dictated the soldier's clothing, task, armament and load more than official scales of issue. For instance, heavy casualties among junior leaders often put a private in command of a section, a sergeant of a platoon, or a lieutenant of a company; in the worst fighting a company might lose all its officers so that command fell entirely upon NCOs. By 1944 Sten guns were in plentiful supply, and privates might acquire them or be issued with them for some tasks, such as patrols or street fighting; at any time senior NCOs might carry binoculars, compasses, flare pistols, torches, etc. In the field officers and men alike might dress themselves to suit the weather and terrain, fighting in shirtsleeves or denims, battle-dress or sweaters.

second lieutenant or lieutenant platoon commander with his radio operator, the platoon sergeant, a 2in mortar with two - man crew, an anti - tank weapon (initially 5.5in Boyes AT rifle, later PIAT projector) with two - man crew, with one or more riflemen runners attached. Three numbered platoons and a command section made up a rifle **company**, of about 125 all ranks, led by a captain or major. By 1944 each **battalion** - of just under 800 all ranks, commanded by a lieutenant-colonel - consisted of four lettered rifle companies; a headquarters company; and a support company with platoons of 3in mortars, towed 6 - pounder anti - tank guns, assault pioneers, and a Bren carrier platoon for rapid deployment. The medium machine gun was not an infantry battalion weapon; Vickers guns were grouped in separate machine gun battalions, of which one was normally assigned to each division of nine infantry battalions.

D - Day, 6 June 1944

The Battle of Normandy opened with the greatest amphibious assault in military history. Had this vast, meticulously planned, but terribly hazardous multi - national operation failed, the history of Europe over the past half century could well have been very different. Before dawn the British 6th and US 82nd and 101st Airborne Divisions had landed by parachute and glider to seize vital points inland and on the flanks of the beachhead. The US 1st Army under General Bradley were to land on the western beaches code- named "Utah" and "Omaha"; the British 2nd Army under General Dempsey were to capture "Gold" and "Sword" beaches, between which lay "Juno", the objective of elements of the 1st Canadian Army under General Crerar.

Here, at H - Hour, 0725, men of the 1st Battalion, The Hampshire Regiment and engineers of a sup- porting Beach Group move towards Gold beach in a Navy - manned Landing Craft Assault. LCAs car- ried about 35 men; they were the smallest craft used to land troops, and the first vessels to hit the beach. The 1st Hampshires, with the 2nd Devonshires and 1st Dorsets, formed 231 Brigade of 50th (Northum- brian) Division; and 231 Brigade was the most westerly British forma- tion to land on D - Day, forming the extreme right flank of 2nd Army. They reached the beach without the planned support of amphibious Sherman DD tanks, most of which were crippled by enemy fire, swamped, bogged down, or landed too far away.

The LCA coxwain, a Royal Navy petty officer, passes the time with a member of the Beach Group, identifiable by his red on white anchor insignia and white helmet band. These Beach Groups were tasked with creating order out of the chaos of an opposed landing by tens of thousands of men; made up of personnel from the Royal Engineers, Royal Electrical & Mechanical Engineers, Royal Army Service Corps, Royal Army Medical Corps and other specialist corps, they salvaged or dragged out of the way any damaged vehicles, cleared tracks, directed traffic, unloaded stores and established dumps, and cared for casualties.

The blue lifebelt worn by the duffle - coated PO was also issued to the Army before the Normandy campaign; it was much in evidence during the Dieppe raid in 1942. It has a small slide - on pocket on the right side which contained a battery unit and light to assist in location at night.

As the landing craft near the beaches enemy fire intensifies. Ahead of the 1st Hampshires, above the beaches round Le Hamel between Arromanches and Courseulles, waits 736 Grenadier Regiment of the Wehrmacht's 716 Division, well fortified in mutually supporting concrete strongpoints behind wire and minefields, and supported by artillery. Beyond the sand dunes lies a marsh and open fields dominated by high ground beyond. This private of the Hampshires has plenty to think about.

For the initial assault wave he is lightly loaded. He wears the utility BD, 37 web equipment in battle order, and the Mk II helmet; and carries a GS shovel and a No 4 rifle with extra ammunition in cotton bandoliers worn over his shoulder. In his small pack are two 24 - hour emergency ration packs issued to the assault troops, who cannot know when they will be resupplied. Troops landing over the beaches later would be more heavily burdened; the 5th Seaforth Highlanders, 51st Division, landed in three feet of water at Courceulles on the afternoon of D+1 carrying the large pack with blanket roll, an extra water-bottle, 2in mortar bombs in improvised hessian "horse collars" round the neck, and wearing cumbersome invasion waders.

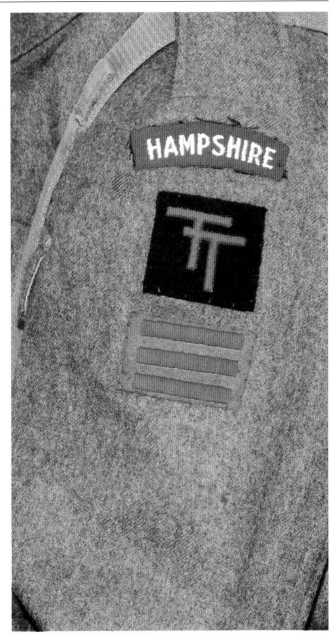

(Right) The Hampshires, who provided battalions for both the Italian and North-West Europe campaigns, were one of the regiments who took it upon themselves to wear special coloured shoulder titles in place of the official black on khaki slip-ons or, in some battalions after 1943, instead of the official white on scarlet titles of the infantry: their title was THE HAMPSHIRE REGT. in yellow on black. As part of the 50th (Northumbrian) Division the 1st Hampshires wore the division's superimposed TT patch in red on black; this recalled the rivers Tyne and Tees, as the 50th was originally formed of units from North-East England; the overlap of the Ts also represented an H for the river Humber, the third major river in the divisional area. The division's 151 Brigade consisted of three battalions of The Durham Light Infantry, and 69 Brigade of one battalion of the East Yorks and two of The Green Howards. Below the divisonal insignia is the scarlet infantry arm of service strip. Officially all such insignia were to be removed before going into battle; in fact, photographs prove that every degree of obedience to this order was to be seen, in Normandy, from completely stripped sleeves to complete arrays of titles, patches and flashes.

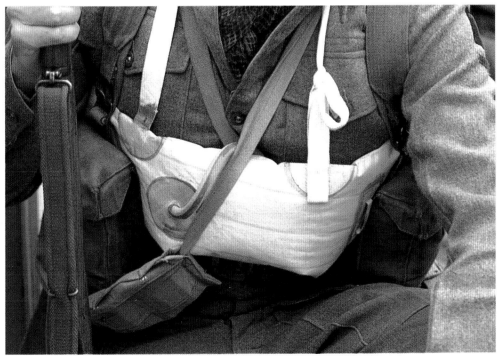

The assault lifebelt was worn partially inflated so as to be less restrictive, beneath any other equipment. If the wearer was unfortunate enough to end up in the sea it would therefore be possible - in theory - to jettison the webbing and other kit and still retain the lifebelt, which could then be fully inflated. The neck strap helped ensure that the belt was worn high, keeping the centre of gravity high and aiding buoyancy. (The Americans suffered casualties with their self-inflating belts, which were frequently worn around the waist and which did not have neck straps; when inflated in the water they sometimes tipped the wearer head down and drowned him.) These lifebelts, jocularly called "water wings", were of fairly flimsy construction and were intended to be dumped as soon as the soldier got his feet on the beach.

(*Above & left*) *H - Hour on Sword beach: elements of No 4 (Army) Commando from Lord Lovat's 1st Special Service Brigade are poised at the waterline, taking cover and beginning to return fire. Along with Commandant Kiefer's Free French Commando and No 6 (Army) Commando, their objective is to take and clear Ouistreham; 6 Cdo will later lead the brigade inland to link up with the 6th Airborne troops who have taken the bridges over the Caen Canal and the river Orne.*

Like their Royal Marine comrades, Army Commandos wore the distinctive green beret, which was more than just headgear - it was the proud mark of a hand - picked elite. Like the red beret of the Airborne Forces, this symbol of esprit de corps was (and still is) worn in the field instead of the helmet whenever possible. It was even argued (against the evidence of exasperated RAMC doctors) that in fact the steel helmet offered as much psychological as practical protection against modern weapons. These men wear no badge on the beret; in June 1944 this was a matter for individual units, as no single Commando cap badge had been fully established. Often the badge of the volunteer's previous regiment or specialist corps was retained.

However, by now shoulder titles had been standardised as red lettering and numerals on a black background for both Army and Royal Marine units; that illustrated, with a red 4 and white COMMANDO, is a surviving earlier design. Beneath the title is the Combined Operations flash introduced in 1942 for personnel of all three services specifically engaged in assaulting the enemy coast.

(Right) Equipment worn on D - Day differed considerably between the Commando units involved. Some troops went into action carrying the Bergen rucksack, as here, of later war manufacture in green canvas. Their large carrying capacity made them suitable for troops who, after taking their objective, might have to hold it unsupported for an extended period before relief arrived. Munitions were somtimes carried in supplementary Pouches, Utility (like pairs of basic pouches issued linked by a neck yoke and waist strap) fixed to attachment straps for them on the rucksack shoulder straps; or in skeleton assault vests. Other Commandos came ashore wearing standard infantry webbing and Mk II helmet. Commandos who had been issued with folding bicycles had the facility to mount their rucksacks onto Everest carriers fixed to the front of their bikes. Toggle ropes for obstacle crossing were also carried by some Commandos.

(Top) The right hand man loads a No 36 grenade into a cup discharger fitted to an SMLE; although obsolete, its role within the platoon having been largely taken over by the 2in mortar, the discharger was still carried by some assault troops in June 1944. Grenades for use with dischargers were fitted with a seven second fuse and a screw - on gas seal plate on the base. The pin was removed and the grenade dropped into the cup, its tight fit holding the safety lever down. The rifle was loaded with a bulletless ballistite round; when fired this projected the grenade to ranges between 80 and 200 yards, the lever springing off and igniting the fuse as soon as the grenade left the cup. Normally within the platoon certain SMLEs would be set aside specifically for use with the discharger, being strengthened against the greater pressure by copper wire bindings around the barrel and forestock and the small of the butt.

(Above) Thomson M1A1 .45 calibre sub - machine gun, purchased from the USA to bridge the gap until the home - produced Sten gun was available in quantity; much used by the Commandos, many of these reliable weapons were retained after the introduction of the flimsier Sten, and they are particularly evident in D - Day photographs.

(Right) *3rd Division medic coming ashore with the assault wave, wearing (at individual choice) a pair of issue "waders" for negotiating the shallows. Anecdotal evidence puts some 50th Division troops in waders for the assault itself; and 51st Division infantry on D+1 were issued waders made of oiled cotton. Ordinarily such boots as these, knee length rubber Wellingtons, etc. were provided to e.g. engineer unit stores for issue as required.*

(Below) *Assembled 08 pattern entrenching tool, re-introduced for use with the 37 pattern web equipment from 1941.*

(Below right) *A private of the 2nd Warwicks, 185 Brigade, 3rd Division (who has picked up a Mk II Sten from a casualty) shelters behind concrete defences while awaiting armoured support; assault battalions of this division wore the new Mk III helmet. At his feet lies a lightweight folding BSA bicycle, as issued to some assault infantry, Commandos and Airborne troops; the idea was that once off the beaches units could use these to break out more quickly for their first day objectives up to 12 miles inland.*

The Division

Divisions committed to the Normandy landings on 6 June 1944 and immediately thereafter were, on Gold beach, 50th (Northumbrian) and 7th Armoured, followed by 49th (West Riding) on D+6; on Sword beach, 3rd Division and 1st Special Service (Commando) Brigade, followed on D+1 by part of 51st (Highland), the rest of which was assigned to follow 3rd Canadian Division and 4th Special Service Brigade ashore on Juno beach.

The **infantry division** in 1944 - 45 fielded between about 17,500 and 18,400 all ranks. Its fighting core was made up of three randomly numbered **infantry brigades**, each of three **battalions** (drawn at random from different named regiments - the infantry regiment had a traditional and administrative identity but was not a battlefield unit). The infantry were supported by a machine gun battalion, three battalion - sized Royal Artillery field regiments, single anti - tank, light anti - aircraft and reconnaissance regiments of battalion size, three Royal Engineer field companies, and many smaller specialist units. Supporting units under Corps or Army command would be attached as needed, e.g. independent tank brigades. Infantry divisions which fought in NW Europe in addition to those mentioned above were 15th (Scottish), 43rd (Wessex), 52nd (Lowland), 53rd (Welsh) and 59th (Staffordshire). The divisions which fought in Italy, 1943 - 45, were the 1st, 4th, 5th, 46th, 56th (London) and 78th.

The basic make - up of an **armoured division** in NW Europe was an **armoured brigade** of three **armoured regiments** (battalion - sized units of tanks) and one **motor battalion** (a half - track infantry battalion, drawn from either the Rifle Brigade or King's Royal Rifle Corps); a lorried **infantry brigade** of three battalions and a support company (medium machine guns and mortars); one towed and one self - propelled field artillery regiments, an AT regiment and an LAA regiment with towed and SP guns; an armoured car regiment, a reconnaissance regiment, and smaller specialist units. Apart from the 7th, the 11th and

Popularly known as the "Bren carrier", the fast, lightly armoured, fully tracked Universal carrier served throughout the war with the carrier platoon of the infantry battalion's HQ company - 13 carriers mounting Brens and one with an anti - tank weapon, carrying 62 all ranks in the rapid deployment and recce roles. The carrier and its later successors were used in practice as all purpose battlefield transport; they might be seen carrying a Vickers machine gun or 3in mortar platoon into battle, towing anti-tank guns, taking hot food or ammunition resupply up to the line, bringing casualties back, or ferrying small numbers of infantry quickly to whererever they were needed - as illustrated by this carrier in the markings of 43rd (Wessex) Division.

Guards Armoured Divisions fought in NW Europe, as did the specialist armoured units of the 79th. The 1st and 6th Armoured Divisions fought in Italy. Divisions marked their vehicles with the same insignia as worn on the troops' shoulder patch, on the near side front and rear; code numbers marked on flashes of different colours on the off side front and rear identified units within a division. Thus the reconnaissance regiments of all infantry divisions bore the code 41 on a green/blue background, as illustrated above. The infantry battalions of the three brigades displayed 55, 56, 57 on red; 60, 61, 62 on green; and 67, 68, 69 on brown, respectively. Within the armoured division, the regiments of the armoured brigade displayed 51, 52, 53 on red, and its motor battalion, 54 on red.

Purely as a representative example, the major units of 43rd (Wessex) Division were: *129 Bde* 4th Bn, Somerset Light Infantry; 4th Bn, Wiltshire Regt; 5th Bn, Wiltshire Regt. *130 Bde* 7th Bn, Hampshire Regt; 4th Bn, Dorsetshire Regt; 5th Bn, Dorsetshire Regt. *214 Bde* 7th Bn, Somerset Light Infantry; 1st Bn, Worcestershire Regt; 5th Bn, Duke of Cornwall's Light Infantry. 43rd Recce Regt, RAC; 94th, 112th, 179th Field Regts.RA; 59th Anti - Tank, 110th Light Anti - Aircraft Regts.RA; and 8th Bn, Middlesex Regt (machine gun battalion).

Assault Jerkins

(Right & opposite) The afternoon of D - Day; on Gold beach two REME sappers of a Beach Group take a rest on their Beach Armoured Recovery Vehicle and discuss with assault infantrymen of The Green Howards from 50th Division the merits of an MP40 sub - machine gun taken from a German prisoner. The role of the BARVs was to clear damaged or broken - down tanks and vehicles under fire, to prevent the vital exit points from the beach becoming blocked; they had an adapted Sherman tank hull minus the turret but with an added armoured superstructure built up to allow them to operate in the shallows without getting swamped.

The Green Howards, unusually for 50th Division troops, have been issued with the assault or battle jerkin of brown duck canvas and webbing. The Battle Jerkin was an experimental design trialed in 1943; the aim was to create a load - carrying system which gave more even distribution of weight rather than being centred on the waistbelt as with the 37 pattern webbing. After tests it was rejected as a general replacement for the web equipment, although some 19,000 were ordered. Its use during the NW Europe campaign was almost entirely limited to D - Day and its immediate aftermath, although it was used to some extent by Commandos in Italy and elsewhere in the Mediterranean theatre. Both British and Canadian assault units wore the jerkin on 6 June, but many seem to have been dumped soon afterwards. Test reports and veterans' memories are mixed in their opinions of it. With its six exterior pockets of different shapes and sizes, and various external loops into which equipment could be slotted, the jerkin could accomodate the same items of kit as the web equipment. The large rear upper pouch served the same function as the small pack, and the lower rear pouch - hanging free on canvas straps - carried the E - tool head. The pouch on the right side carried the water bottle; that on the left side could be used for various munitions, as could both upper front pouches - Bren magazines, grenades or 2in mortar bombs. The rifle bayonet scabbard and E - tool haft fitted through loops on the exterior of the left side and upper rear pouches respectively. There was a pocket inside the right chest; and another large one across the inside of the lower back, for "soft kit" only.

(Left) Rear view of a jerkin produced in tan fabric - these are marked for training use only. The ground sheet/ cape projects from below the flap of the upper back pouch; the machete scabbard is fed through the canvas sleeve on the right of the pouch. Machetes were normally carried by the section NCO or Bren group commander; most had leather scabbards and bakelite grips, but there are examples of rigid fibre scabbards and of grips made of wood or leather. Battle jerkins were produced in small, medium and large sizes, these words being marked on the khaki cotton lining of the shoulder area; the black stencilled words SOFT KIT are also found across the lining at bottom rear, indicating that only soft items were to be packed closest to the body in the inside bottom pocket.

(Above) The carrying positions of the No 4 bayonet and E - tool haft are visible; and note the cord loop and wooden toggle fastening of all pouches. The jerkin was closed by web straps and tongueless brass buckles at chest and waist. This Bren crew No 1 has the spare parts wallet slung over the jerkin to hang at his left side. Unlike the 3rd Division, most 50th Division troops still wore the Mk II helmet; here the chin strap is worn pulled up over the brim in case of shell blast - this could lift the helmet sharply, injuring the jaw or neck if the strap were worn under the chin.

Street Fighting: KOSB in Caen

(Left) *June 1944: two soldiers of the 1st Battalion, King's Own Scottish Borderers advance cautiously through shattered ruins on the outskirts of the ancient Norman city of Caen, which will be devastated by Allied bombardment and will suffer great loss of civilian life before the British finally capture it. One "Kosbie" is pulling the pin from a No 36 grenade, a weapon used to good effect and in large numbers in the murderous and costly hide - and - seek of street fighting. His rifleman teammate covers him at all times, while staying alert to avoid grenade fragments himself. The bomber wears the utility BD as it appeared from mid - 1942, with unpleated pockets and exposed front buttons. Typically of many units in France at this time he wears full insignia, including the Leslie tartan flash which replaced a regimental title in the KOSB, the 3rd Division patch, and two scarlet infantry strips to indicate 9 Brigade - since their introduction in September 1940 units within infantry divisions had been authorised to wear either one, two or three strips to indicate whether their battalion served in the senior, intermediate or junior of the three brigades. Both soldiers wear the Mk III "turtle" helmet issued to most of the 3rd Division assault troops who stormed Sword beach on D - Day. It was an improvement over the Mk II, its shape offering better protection from the side and rear. The liner was the same as that used in the Mk II; as with the earlier liners, it was retained by a nut and bolt through the apex of the skull.*

(Above) In addition to grenades, light automatic weapons were also ideal for the close confines and snap shooting of street fighting. The 9mm Mk III Sten, with its welded metal tube body, was a cheaper version of the already very utilitarian Mk II weapon. Weighing a little under 7lb and with a rate of fire of 550rpm, it was a handy weapon even though it was not initially appreciated by those issued with it. Its cheapness and crudity of manufacture earned it the nickname of the "Woolworths gun" amongst other less printable titles. The weapon soon proved its worth, however: it was effective at the short battle ranges for which it was built; and as long as the user avoided damaging the magazine feed lips lest they cause jams, and was careful not to knock the cocking handle free of its rudimentary safety slot, it performed well. It was available in very large numbers, and was carried by many infantry officers and NCOs, vehicle crews, and other personnel whose duties made the rifle inconveniently bulky.

(Above right) The first pattern loading tool shown fitted to a Sten magazine; this type, with its brass lever, was first issued with the Lanchester SMG, relegated to Royal Navy and RAF use after acceptance of the Sten. It was replaced by the simpler Mk II tool; both enabled 32 rounds to be fed into the magazine with relative ease.

(Right) The rifleman's bayonet No 4 Mk II. The Spike bayonet was introduced with the No 4 rifle to replace the old No 1 (P1907) bayonet that had been used with the SMLE. The bayonet came in four patterns: the Mk I had a cruciform section blade, the Mk II had a plain oval section blade, the Mk II* was similar to the Mk II but had a distinct join where the blade met the socket, and the Mk III had a very crudely finished socket. The No 4 bayonet at left is shown with a "Frog, Bayonet, WE 37", as originally issued with the No 1 bayonet, but with an added "Tab, Securing, Bayonet" for use with the No 4 bayonet scabbard. At right is a modified frog with a slit cut into the upper loop, allowing fitting of the scabbard boss.

(**Above & left**) In the temporary refuge of a French family's ruined home, the two Jocks snatch a brief opportunity to rest, catch up on news - and prime grenades for their next battle... As a Scottish regiment the KOSB wore the tam o'shanter, officially termed the Balmoral bonnet, instead of the FS and later GS caps when in the field (the Glengarry was worn as the equivalent of the coloured FS cap). The cap badge was supposedly worn with a backing patch of Leslie tartan, although this rule was often ignored. For a soldier who has endured some of the hardest fighting of the Normandy campaign to date the dangers of smoking while screwing the igniter set (detonator, exposed fuse, cap chamber and percussion cap) into a 36 grenade seem to be regarded as negligible.

(Above) For front line troops a newspaper, no matter how old, provided a welcome glimpse of the world beyond their slit trench. For many the treatment of Allied victories provided a little wry comic relief; but for others the news stories provided them with more information about their units' achievements than their own superiors ever did. Ever cautious, this soldier keeps his No 4 rifle close at hand; its muzzle is kept clean by his TOS, with its quilted lining and tartan badge backing.

(Right) The generously cut "tammie" could be adjusted for size to some extent by an overlap at the rear of the headband secured by a tape, normally tied in a neat bow which was then occasionally stitched in place.

(Bottom right) Box of a dozen No 36 grenades laid out for priming on a captured German Zeltbahn. Igniter sets were packed separately in three - set tins, four of these red - painted tins being packed in the central compartment of the box. The time delay of the fuses was marked in yellow on the top of the box: four seconds for hand grenades, which had a white fuse with a paper or rubber band which could be felt in the dark, and seven seconds for rifle grenades, which had a yellow fuse without a band. (For obvious safety reasons the fuse and detonator shown here are dummies.)

Windproof Camouflage Suit

(Left) This sniper wears the camouflage version of the windproof smock and trousers; in cut these followed the general pattern of all windproof clothing. The smock was a popular garment among such specialist troops, but was also on general issue towards the end of the war, being widely seen in photographs of infantry. (Denison smocks and captured German items of SS spotted and Wehrmacht splinter camouflage pattern also saw use among British troops.) While this windproof suit had an excellent camouflage base, individual snipers often made up their own "ghillie" suits using hessian scrim, netting, or any other available fabrics that would help blend in with their environment. Camouflage face veils - 3ft x 3ft 6in nets, dyed in a grass green and brown pattern - were a general issue item. They were intended for spreading over the helmet, shoulders and pack to break up the outline against observation from the air or ground. Many soldiers wore them as scarfs in the opened neck of the BD blouse.

(**Left & below**) The rifle No 4 Mk I*(T). Snipers' rifles were selected weapons, chosen for their tighter than average grouping; a cheek piece was added to the butt and the receiver was modified to take the No 32 telescopic sight, graduated to 1,000 yards. The US M1907 leather sling was standard issue for this weapon, since it made a better adjustable arm brace than the British web sling. Snipers were deployed to dominate the ground between the lines during the brief periods of fairly static confrontation.

Typical sniper's accoutrements included a compass, a telescope or binoculars, maps and mapcase, and a protective metal case for the No 32 telescopic sight.

(**Left**) Windproof camouflage suit worn by a crewman from a Bren carrier, who is adjusting track tension using the rod and tensioning tool provided. By winter 1944 - 45 this camouflage clothing was not limited to special forces or troops with specialist duties; for instance, photographs show it widely worn by infantrymen of 131 Brigade, 7th Armoured Division. The labels applied to the range of windproof smocks are, as already noted, often contradictory and confusing, depending on manufacturer: camouflage smocks were often not marked as such; and the drab and white smocks often bear the description "Smock, Camouflaged".

Vickers Section

In 1944 medium machine gun companies of 16 guns might be attached to an infantry battalion. The divisional machine gun battalion had 48 .303in Vickers guns - an elderly and complex design, but very reliable and long - ranging. Apart from direct fire at a visible enemy the Vickers in its sustained fire role was capable of putting down devastating indirect fire, creating a "beaten zone" at ranges out to two miles. MG units were motorised, initially with the ubiquitous 15cwt truck and later in Universal carriers. Each of the four MMGs in a platoon would need two carriers to bring the gun, ammunition and crew into action.

(Left) The 50lb tripod cradle with elevating and traversing mechanism is carried by the crew No 1, with the aid of a thick felt and leather shoulder pad. No 2 carried the 42lb gun itself, and the clino sight in its metal protective box. Certain converted infantry regiments (e.g. the Middlesex, Manchesters, Cheshires and Kensingtons) provided many of the MG battalions for divisions in NW Europe; these men are from the 1/7th Middlesex, 51st (Highland) Division, wearing the HD patch in red on navy blue - a variant of the normal red on medium blue, locally produced during the unit's service in North Africa.

(Above) Having "de - bussed" well to the rear the section advances on foot over the "short carry" to its positions, since vehicle noise and dust tended to alert the enemy. Adopting single file to lessen the ever - present danger from enemy anti - personnel mines, the crews follow a point man armed with a Sten who is scouting well ahead of the section. A well - worn track like this would generally be avoided as being too obvious a target.

(Above & above right) *An ammunition number carries the condenser can, used to collect water evaporated off from the barrel jacket as it becomes heated; it could then be recycled. The adjustable web straps attached to his pouches are a part of the "liner carrier" worn on his back. The web carrier could hold two ammunition box "liners", factory - sealed tins each holding a 250 - round belt; it was less tiring than hand - carrying them in boxes, and left the hands free for weapons and other equipment.*

(Right) *The platoon commander, acting as fire controller for the section, checks the lay of the guns using his prismatic compass and map board. From his calculations a number of predetermined fire tasks can be plotted, and targets engaged day or night, in much the same way as artillery engage their targets. Accuracy of calculation was aided by the rangefinder and mathematical instruments such as slide rules and protractors. The effectiveness of any fire task would depend greatly upon the individual skills of the fire controller.*

(Left) For direct fire on targets within visual range the gun was sighted up to 4,000 yards using the tangent sight. For indirect fire the gun was aimed using the dial sight - as here - the tangent sight being folded flat. The dial sight, used with aiming posts during the day and aiming lamps at night, allowed the gunner to engage targets that were out of sight such as those in dead ground. The aiming posts - see in background - were normally placed to the front left of the gun if terrain permitted.

(Right) Ammunition was supplied in 250 - round woven fabric belts with riveted brass spacers, stored in sealed metal liners held in wooden boxes with integral carrying handles. For action the liner was ripped open along prepared seams using a pull ring, and the gun's No 2 fed the belt's brass leader into the right of the action; spent cartridge cases were ejected below the weapon, and the empty belt fed out from the left side of the breech.

(Above) The Vickers in action - note flame in parabolic flash deflector fitted to this gun, a device which reduced the tell - tale muzzle flash, particularly when viewed from a flank. The theoretical rate of fire was in excess of 450 rounds per minute, although in practice one 250 - round belt was fired in two minutes (one belt per minute for rapid fire).

(Right) Stood down: a Vickers crew clean and maintain their gun. With the action stripped down and the barrel removed worn components can be replaced or adjusted as required, and a thorough cleaning and lubrication helps ensure smooth operation. The spare parts wallet contains over 30 items, from tools to replacement components, and another 136 items are kept in the wooden spare parts box - a skilled crew can rectify most defects in the field. Note that the No 1 wears here a khaki woollen balaclava rolled up as a cap comforter.

(Left) Barr & Stroud rangefinder; dating from the earliest days of the Vickers gun, this was an essential instrument allowing the platoon to obtain accurate ranges for reference points and targets. Alongside it lies the standard Mk II steel helmet showing the second pattern, cruciform rubber skull pad.

(Below) While vital maintenance is carried out on one of the section's guns the second remains loaded and ready for action; just as with an infantry section's small arms, it was bad practice to clean all weapons at once.

(Above) To ensure the barrel remained cool it was essential that the barrel jacket was kept full of water. During sustained fire the water rapidly boiled off down the condenser tube into the 2 - gallon water can - about 500 - 600 rounds were enough to boil it. Some steam was always lost before it could be recycled, and the water had to be replaced; if there was no other immediate water source the crew would empty their water bottles into the jacket; in real emergencies urine provided a practical if antisocial alternative.

(Right) This "hostilities only" second lieutenant is the platoon commander; his rank is indicated by the single "pip" or star on his epaulettes, in pale worsted thread on a backing of red infantry arm - of - service colour. His officer status is immediately visible from his opened utility pattern BD blouse revealing a collar and tie. Despite a specific prohibition in King's Regulations para 1005, this officer's watchchain is visibly suspended from the second buttonhole to the breast pocket of his blouse - such trinkets were not to be visible, but in the field individual whims and practicality were of greater concern than regulations. He wears the officer's 37 pattern web set, with the waterbottle slung over the shoulder on a separate spare brace. His weapon is the 9mm Mk II Sten with 32 - round box magazine, but he also carries a .38 Enfield revolver.

Much of a soldier's life was spent out of action, allowing time to prepare food and make any necessary repairs to his kit. When conditions permitted hot food cooked in bulk was brought forward from the unit rear echelons to feed whole companies at a time. Otherwise rations were prepared by the individual, by a few mates, or by a section together. From 1943 "compo" rations were introduced: wooden boxes containing enough tinned rations to feed 14 men three different meals in a day, with seven different menus available. These were generally popular; they contained solid meals of meat and vegetables and good stodgy puddings, with thinner, relatively softer Army biscuits, jams, cheese, and such comforts as tea, chocolate, boiled sweets, cigarettes and toilet paper. The tins were small, which made division between the section easy; all heating could be done by piercing the tins and dropping them in boiling water, unless soldiers preferred to mix up the contents.

(Right) Minor repairs to uniform were made by the individual; more seriously damaged clothing was repaired by the battalion tailors, or handed in to the Quartermaster for exchange. The issue grey wool socks were particularly prone to wear and needed frequent darning to prolong their useful life - a skill hard learned by the average 1940s soldier, who was most unlikely to have had to look after himself in civvy street, coming straight from a home shared with his mother, sisters or wife.

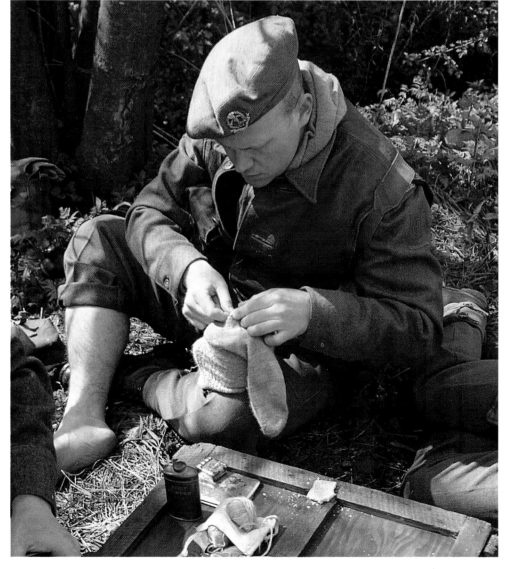

(Opposite top) Mess tins and rations. Two patterns of tinned steel mess tin are illustrated, the early type having an embossed ridge around the tin to mark 1 pint; this was deleted from later production. Each man was issued a knife, fork and spoon, but the first two were often discarded - the spoon and issue clasp knife were generally sufficient to manage most meals. Here a privately acquired stove is being used. Many commercial types were seen, usually burning spirits or fuel vapour pumped under pressure. This was the method used for an issue stove, of which one or more per vehicle were provided to motorised troops. From 1944 a simple individual cooker was issued; this had folding iron vanes which packed flat or opened to make a trivet for a mess tin or mug, with a cut - out section below for a solid fuel tablet. (All individual heaters, issue or commercial, were invariably called "tommy cookers", so that phrase is an unreliable identification for a particular type.) Motorised troops who had space to carry them invariably made "desert cookers" out of a petrol tin cut in half: petrol was mixed into earth or sand and lighted in the bottom tin, and water, tea, sugar and tinned milk were brewed up together in the second tin placed over the flames. Veterans swear that this liquid won the war.

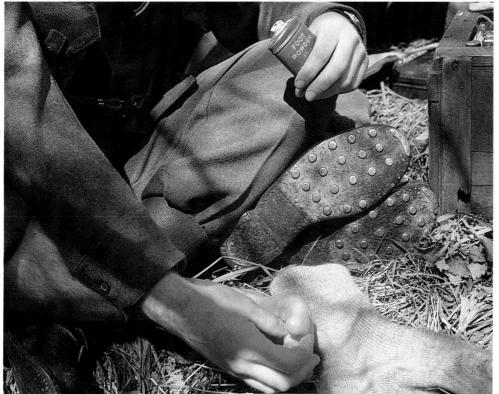

(Above) The issue "housewife" (pronounced "hussif") was the soldier's only weapon in the constant battle to keep his clothing in good repair. It contained all the necessary needles, buttons, thread and wool to make minor repairs to the different garments which he wore; a brass thimble was also included, later replaced by a black plastic economy model.

(Left) Having darned his socks he takes time to ensure that his feet are clean and free from blisters, and applies a generous dusting of issue foot powder. Note the horseshoe and stud arrangement of the ammunition boots; as an economy measure the number of studs or "hobs" was to be progressively reduced as the years passed, from 25 to 13 per boot, and the four screws securing the toe plate were also reduced to three. Constant maintenance was required, as studs and plates were easily lost on hard ground and any omissions resulted in direct wear on the leather sole.

Glider Infantry

The term "Airborne" is often mistakenly understood as applying only to parachute units; but in World War II it included substantial numbers of troops of several arms of service who were delivered to their objective by gliders - a hazardous method, costly in lives and abandoned after its brief vogue in 1941 - 45 . A complete infantry brigade and virtually all the supporting arms and services of a British airborne division came into this category of air - landing forces. Airborne troops were readily identifiable by several items of dress and equipment which were unique to them, although as the war progressed this became less the case.

(**Left**) This private of the 2nd Bn, The Oxfordshire & Buckinghamshire Light Infantry is a member of 6 Air - Landing Brigade, 6th Airborne Division. The "Ox & Bucks" were one of several infantry battalions converted en bloc to the air - landing role; the others in 6 Brigade were the 1st Royal Ulster Rifles and 12th Devons. The 2nd Ox & Bucks recorded their most notable sucess on the night of 5/6 June 1944 when, in the very first moments of the Allied liberation of Europe, six platoons landed by glider to capture and hold the vital bridges over the river Orne and the Caen Canal. (Glider - borne infantry were paid an extra shilling a day - 10p - in recognition of the risks they faced.)

His appearance typifies that of the Airborne soldier; the most distinctive item of dress is his Smock, Denison, Airborne Forces, with its printed camouflage pattern and half - length front zip. Note the seven pocket webbing Bandolier, Sten; made from 1942, this freed the basic pouches for other essentials such as grenades. Kit stowage space was at a premium for Airborne troops, who required a high degree of self - sufficiency as there was no guarantee of early resupply once they were behind enemy lines.

(**Opposite top**) Third pattern Airborne helmet, here with the web chin straps which began to replace the earlier leather type from 1944. The straps had a leather cup section for the chin and a long nape strap that ran through a loop at the rear of the helmet, giving a more secure fit, particularly when parachuting. Note the heavily padded rim and crown pad, and the web cradle supporting the helmet on the wearer's crown. Ballistic protection was comparable to the general issue Mk II helmet, although the higher and more vertical sides of the Airborne helmet reduced the "glancing" effect. To break up the outline hessian scrim has been added to the helmet net.

(Left) Mk V Sten gun - a refinement of the Mk II, with a wooden stock, pistol grips, a foresight and provision for fitting the bayonet of the No 4 rifle. The "improvements" were in fact questionable, increasing the weight without markedly improving the functioning of the weapon.

(Right) The Mk II loading tool fitted to the Sten's 32 - round box magazine; this eased the loading of the magazine by holding the rounds down against the internal spring so that additional rounds could be dropped in rather than forced in against the spring.

Body Armour & Trousers, Parachutist

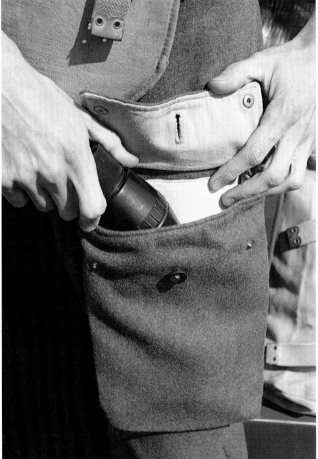

(*Above left & above*) Summer 1944: this Airborne soldier, waiting on an English airfield for one of the many operations which were planned only to be cancelled at the last minute, wears a set of the body armour which had ben introduced into service in 1942. Despite being relatively lightweight the armour was not popular due to its discomfort and the slight loss of mobility. Nevertheless, 79,000 sets were issued to 21st Army Group, the Royal Air Force, and various smaller organisations; and 12,000 of these went to the 1st and 6th Airborne Divisions. The armour was designed to protect the most vital areas of the body from low velocity impacts such as shrapnel from shells and mortar bombs. A webbing harness supported a chest plate with a slightly smaller abdominal plate suspended from it; a shaped plate provided protection across the small of the back and the kidney area. High velocity projectiles, including rifle calibre bullets, would penetrate and possibly fragment the armour, causing additional injury; but since such impacts to the unprotected body would be at least equally serious and often fatal, the advantages of wearing the armour outweighed the disadvantages. Such logical reasoning does not always convince soldiers, however.

Note in the rear view the Trousers, Parachutist, issued to Airborne Forces; these have two rear dressing pockets in addition to the conventional one on the front of the right hip.

(*Left*) The Trousers, Parachutist, had the side and left thigh pockets lined with chamois leather for extra strength. The thigh pocket was of expanding type, with a flap secured by a button and two press studs. It would take a far greater load than the conventional BD map pocket, and could easily hold three grenades - such as the bakelite No 69 blast grenade illustrated.

Medical Orderly

Because their operations often left them isolated, each brigade of an Airborne division had its own unit of the Royal Army Medical Corps; e.g., 1 Air - Landing Brigade, 1st Airborne Division (1st Border Regt, 2nd South Staffords, 7th KOSB) had under command 181 Field Ambulance RAMC.

The "red" - maroon - beret was approved as distinguishing headgear for all members of Airborne Forces in summer 1942 shortly after formation of The Parachute Regiment, at the same time as the introduction of a number of Airborne insignia in claret and Cambridge blue - the horseracing colours of Maj.Gen. Browning, commander of the fledgeling 1st Airborne Division. Qualified members of Airborne Forces wore their own regimental or corps badges on the beret: here, a wartime economy plastic version of the RAMC badge.

This medical orderly of an air - landing field ambulance wears the Denison smock over general issue battledress, third pattern Airborne helmet, and 37 pattern webbing; the basic pouches would be used for extra medical supplies rather than ammunition by unarmed RAMC personnel, and he has a red cross brassard on his right arm. Extra field dressings are tied to his smock epaulettes; this was common practice among Airborne troops and the Commandos who acquired the Denison later in the war, as the dressing was more accessible there than in the front hip pocket of a wounded man wearing the long smock and heavy belt order.

(Below) As well as the small pack, E - tool, and toggle rope the medic also carries a small medical field pack containing an assortment of dressings and instruments such as scissors and tourniquets for immediate use. Normally the orderly would be working with others and would have access to the larger field medical pack, which would equip him to provide most types of field emergency treatment.

(Below right) The "donkey tail" of the Denison smock could be passed between the wearer's legs and fastened at the front with press studs to prevent the smock riding up during a parachute descent; it was superfluous when the smock was worn by glider troops, and Denisons are often seen with the tail cut off.

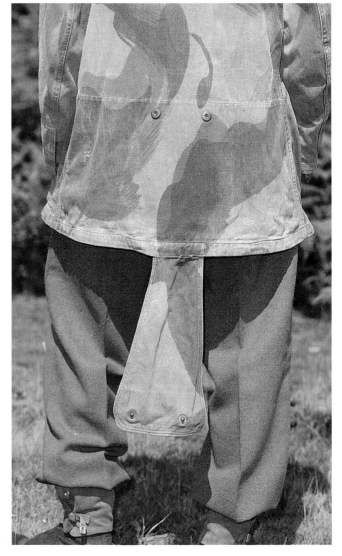

(Left) Because of the isolated nature of Airborne operations the medical support had to be of the highest standard. Regimental Aid Posts were the first point of assistance for the wounded; treatment here consisted mainly of arresting haemorrhaging, dressing wounds, and stabilisation of the patient ready for transfer out of the combat zone. Being the most forward medical posts RAPs were always in danger from enemy action, including small arms fire, and were frequently overrun during fluid battlefield situations. Enemy wounded were treated alongside our own men - the RAMC (and their Wehrmacht counterparts) categorised casualties by the severity and urgency of their wounds, not by nationality.

(Right) An orderly tends to a badly wounded soldier using instruments from the field medical pack; a tourniquet has been applied to the left upper arm to restrict bleeding while the wound is attended to. The quality of this initial treatment would often determine the patient's chances of survival; thanks to recent advances which made available penicillin, sulpha drugs and transfusion with stored plasma, these were good under most circumstances, including a surprisingly high proportion even of head and abdominal wounds. (Their isolation condemned Airborne casualties to markedly lower rates of recovery, however.) Note that the left hand orderly - rigging up a plasma bottle to replace vital fluids, and reduce the degree of shock following blood loss - has a Fairbairn Sykes Commando knife sheathed inside the special leg seam pocket of the Airborne trousers.

(Left) Having stopped all bleeding and stabilised the wounded Tommy as well as possible he is prepared for the move back down the line, and eventual return to a hospital at home. Those needing the most urgent specialist treatment were the first to be moved back down the chain of medical services. Here the orderlies move the casualty using a lightweight folding pattern Stretcher, Airborne, supported by a shoulder harness; for moving a casualty any distance each stretcher required four bearers. The normal route was from a Regimental Aid Post, to an Advance Dressing Station, to a Casualty Clearing Station, and eventually to a Main Hospital. This was not a simple procedure at the best of times, and for Airborne casualties evacuation to a hospital had to wait until air extraction was possible or the ground forces advanced to link up.

Tented Bivouac

(Right) Even the intelligently assembled compo rations got monotonous after a while, with only seven menus of tinned food to provide variety. Like soldiers since the dawn of history, Tommies were always on the look - out for something fresher to purchase, barter or otherwise acquire. This contented private returns triumphant with the essential element of a really spectacular supper under his arm.

He is wearing the Jerkin, Leather, which had its origins in the Great War and was in general use throughout World War II. Collarless, sleeveless and pocketless, it was sized so that it could fit comfortably over the battledress, and it was not unknown for it to be worn over the greatcoat. It had four plastic buttons down the front and was lined in battledress or similar khaki - green fabric, although some 1945 examples have dark brown and dark green linings. As the war progressed the construction of jerkins became more "patchwork" so as not to waste the smaller off - cuts of leather. Popularly conceived as being for MT drivers, despatch riders and artillerymen in particular - i.e., categories of troops whose duties exposed them to the weather but who needed greater freedom of movement than offered by the greatcoat - jerkins were not an item of workwear, and were in fact widely issued to troops of all arms as an alternative to the greatcoat during cold conditions.

(Left) Bright and eager for the new day, a soldier emerges from his bivouac and eyes the nearest bushes, entrenching tool in hand. He is sporting Vest and Drawers, Cellular, the lighter weight set of Army issue underwear; the pullover vest has a round neck with two cloth - covered buttons on the front placket. Protruding from the top of his boots are grey woollen issue socks. Around his neck hang the two identity disks worn at all times by all personnel. The entrenching tool haft with a fitting for the spike bayonet was not widely seen until late in the NW Europe campaign.

(Below) Supper is disassembled in a brisk and soldierly manner. Despite misgivings about accommodating men in pairs only, the bivouac tent came into use from 1942. Typically in dark brown or tan canvas, it requires nine wooden pegs and has two square - section wooden upright poles. There are two flaps at each end, though the rear flaps project to provide extra space. At the front and rear mosquito net is stitched in so that the flaps can be opened for ventilation without letting in insects (mosquitoes were a plague in summer not only in Italy but also in Normandy). There are pockets along the interior of the lower sides of the tent, which can be filled with rocks or sand to weigh them down and keep out draughts. The canvas is not proofed, and water will pass through if the inside surface is disturbed. Although a small kit bag in which to pack the tent was manufactured, the poles are too long to fit inside it. The bivouac tent was at the bottom end of a range of tentage used by the Army in the field, up to marquee size; some of these were produced in camouflaged material.

(Above) Every soldier wore a pair of pressed fibre identity "discs", one hexagonal in dull green and one round in brick red; both bore his name, regimental number and religion. In the event of death the green disc was to be left on the corpse to aid its future identification by the Graves Registration detail; the red disc, usually worn on a separate string loop, was to be removed and handed in to unit clerical staff. Individuals sometimes replaced the issue thin cord with a chain or leather thong, and might add personal good luck charms or keepsakes. The discs shown here identified 5724674 Pearcey, H., Church of England. The regimental number identifies him as belonging to The Dorsetshire Regiment, 5718001 to 5763000 being allocated to that regiment under Army Order 49 of 1926. Appendix XIX of King's Regulations gave a full listing of all units and allotted numbers. Personal numbering for soldiers dated back to 1829 when a system was introduced whereby each unit numbered its own men; in August 1920 the new block system replaced this.

No 18 Radio Set

The Wireless Set No 18 was a general purpose man - portable radio carried by infantry units down to platoon level.

It had an output of .5 watt with a frequency band of 6.0 to 9.0 megacycles. As a mobile unit it had a range of between two and six miles; in its stationary role the range could be increased to eight miles. Its total weight was around 35lbs. The WS38 and WS48 were developments of the 18 set (the designation number of each subsequent development being increased by 10.)

(Right) The two component units of the WS18 set. The upper unit is the receiver and the lower the transmitter; they were essentially separate units contained in one housing. The battery was contained in the lower section of the case, and access required removing the transmitter unit. The waterproof canvas cover gave some protection to the electrical components; when the set was not in use the cover and its metal flaps could be closed over the face of the radio.

(Below) The WS18 in use as a mobile unit: a platoon commander communicates with his company commander. Two headsets were required, one for the signaller and one for use by other operators with a microphone. Note that the webbing headset harness was designed for use beneath a steel helmet. Additional parts, including spare valves and a morse key, were carried in the Satchel, Signals, worn on the left hip. Extra copper aerial sections are attached to the side of the set; the use of all the sections at once was impractical in the mobile role.

Bren Group

Autumn 1944: taking cover in a drainage ditch somewhere in the Low Countries, the Bren team of an infantry section lay down covering fire for riflemen during "fire and movement" - their key role. The Bren, here with bipod down and carrying handle folded over, has an effective range of up to 1,500 yards; the magazine holds - in practice - 28 rounds. The No 1 and No 2 carry about a dozen magazines in their basic and utility pouches, and others are distributed among the rest of the section. The junior NCO points out targets to the No 1; tracer rounds can be used to highlight the point of aim. Ready to change magazines - or barrels every 500 rounds, by lifting the release latch on the left of the receiver ahead of the magazine - the No 2 crouches to the gunner's right. He wears an extra pair of utility pouches; these can also carry 2in mortar bombs for another of the platoon's support weapons. All unit insignia have been removed here for security; the only badge visible is the No 1's LG qualification on the left forearm (originally for Lewis Gunner).

(Left) This action over, the No 2 passes the Bren up to his No 1. The web sling, slighty longer than a rifle's, attaches by two strong spring clips to mounting eyes on the gun. On his back the No 2 carries the spare barrel bag or "holdall" (here in web, although others exist in khaki canvas). The main bag carries the spare barrel and a sectional cleaning rod. Small external pockets hold various cleaning heads for the rod, a bottle of graphited grease and a plastic bottle of cold weather oil. The largest external pocket holds the spare parts wallet. This contains an oil bottle, barrel pull - through with double loop, a combination tool, and the spare parts tin with fouling tool, cleaning gauzes, and springs and other replaceable parts (essential items might be duplicated in both the wallet and the holdall, for safety). The colour contrast here makes it easy to distinguish the utility pouches worn on his chest above the basic pouches. Empty sandbags for future use are tucked with the ground sheet under the haversack flap.

(Right) Out of the line, an experienced crew take any opportunity for cleaning and basic maintenance. The Bren is field - stripped on a blanket (to prevent loss of smaller parts) - a quick and easy process involving only half a dozen main components. The No 1 has both barrels out for pulling through and oiling; here he cleans the gas port with the fouling tool, while his mate oils the bipod. Laid out are the rest of the main components: by his knee the receiver with magazine housing, in the foreground the butt and trigger assembly. On the blanket note the open spare parts tin, and the single locking pin which holds the entire assembly together.

(Above) The spares wallet lies open at left foreground; with oil bottles and flannel "four by two" cleaning cloth the crew work on the return rod in the butt and trigger group, and the sight drum on the receiver.

(Right) The No 2 refills empty magazines and packs them. Cartridges come packed in cardboard boxes, sealed in 250-round tin liners like those used for MG belts, and carried in the same brown-painted plywood outer boxes. In the foreground are metal cases for 12 loaded magazines, which would be carried in unit transport ready for distribution of magazines to LMG teams and section riflemen. At left is a subdivided brown canvas sling bag for carrying extra magazines - this only came into use towards the end of the war.

Tank Oversuit &
Denim Tank Suit

(Below) First seeing widespread issue in 1943, the Oversuit, Tank Crews (more popularly, the "Pixie suit") was a warm and practical garment, obviously based upon the design of the 1942 tank suit. The suit was made from heavyweight tan cotton with a full interior lining of khaki wool fabric. It had seven external patch pockets, two side pockets with vents allowing access to clothing worn beneath, and three internal pockets. Ankles and wrists had adjustment tabs, the wrists also having elasticated internal cuffs. The tall, lined collar could be closed around the face with a double strap and buckle arrangement. Getting into and out of the oversuit was made easier by two full length zips running from the throat down each side of the chest and continuing down each leg to terminate at the ankle.

Due to the weight of the suit it was provided with integral supporting braces; these ran from the rear waist, through cloth channels over the shoulders and down to adjustable buckles inside the front waist. Designed to distribute the weight slightly better, they were frequently removed from the suit, as was the external waistbelt.

(Top) Strengthened epaulettes were fitted at each shoulder, secured with press studs. The cloth was strong enough for them to be used in the extraction of a wounded man, but their general lack of bulk made a firm grip very difficult, and only a very strong man would have been able to drag the dead weight of a casualty from a tank using the epaulettes alone. Unlike the 1942 suit the oversuit had no internal rescue harness.

The Royal Armoured Corps pattern steel helmet was an improvement over the earlier fibre types, offering both considerably greater crash protection and, unlike its predecessors, ballistic protection as well. The shell was the same as that used for the despatch rider's and Mk III Airborne helmets, the three differing only in their liners. The RAC helmet used the same type of liner as the Mk II general service helmet.

(Above) A hood, of the same fabric as the suit, could be attached at the collar using five press studs.

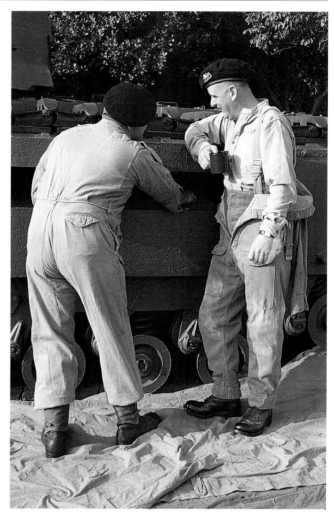

(Above) Dismounting from his Churchill tank, this trooper of one of the RAC regiments formed from battalions of The King's Own Royal Regiment wears the tanker's black beret with the lion badge of his old infantry unit. His overall is the Tank Suit, Denim - essentially a light denim version of the heavy canvas oversuit opposite. It had fewer pockets - only six external, two side and one internal; two of the internal and both shin pockets were deleted when compared with the heavier suit. There were no zips; a fly front opening ran from the neck to the crotch, secured by the same composition buttons as used on the pockets and epaulettes. There was no provision for a hood. A waistbelt was provided but was often discarded.

(Above right) As with the oversuit, the denim suit had integral braces. Designed to run through channels at the shoulders, they were often unthreaded from these so that they ran straight over the shoulders, thereby allowing the upper part of the suit to be dropped to the waist while still being supported by the braces. This view shows these adjustable internal braces, and the rear hip pocket unique to this denim version of the tank suit.

(Right) Seated on the turret of a Sherman examining a captured Fallschirmjäger helmet, this Royal Tank Regiment trooper wears the headset to the No 19 radio set, and has the hand - held microphone tucked in the pocket of his denim suit. The No 19 was a general purpose radio with a range of up to 20 miles; it was standard in British tanks, and in many other vehicles. At his side is the black first aid outfit for armoured fighting vehicles which, as stated on the lid, was an outside component kept in an external stowage bin.

Reconnaissance Corps

The Reconnaissance Corps was formed in 1941, with the role of providing advance intelligence of enemy positions and movements for infantry divisions - a task previously undertaken by cavalry units. In January 1944 the Reconnaissance Corps became part of the Royal Armoured Corps, officially adopting the black beret as from that time. Typically, units were generally slow to discard their old headgear, and the khaki beret was still to be seen as late as January 1945.

(Above) Officers and men of C Squadron, 43rd Reconnaissance Regiment - the recce asset of 43rd (Wessex) Infantry Division - pause during the division's long fighting advance through France and the Low Countries into Germany. The unit medical officer, at left, wears an issue sleeveless leather jerkin which has been modified by the addition of two front pockets, a collar, and epaulettes all in leather - typical of the private conversions carried out for many officers. At right, a trooper wears an even more radically modified jerkin, with a collar and sleeves added from an issue greatcoat; this makes a very warm garment considerably less restrictive than a greatcoat when worn in an armoured vehicle.

(Left) This subaltern wears the officer's silver and gilt badge on green backing on a private purchase khaki beret; bronze finish badges, as worn on the SD cap, were also worn on the beret. The pattern of the camouflaged version of the sleeveless leather jerkin is very evident here; the finish was applied by paint spray at the factory producing the garments.

(Above) *Beret, Basque - the khaki version as worn by the Reconnaissance Corps and the infantry of Motor Battalions from October 1942; it was also authorised for wear with BD by all officers from the rank of colonel upwards from September 1943. (In 1944 many more junior officers of other arms of service tried to get away with wearing them, against specific orders, after the official introduction of the despised GS cap.) It bears here the economy plastic pattern of the Corps' spear and lightnings cap badge.*

(Above right) *As he is attached to a Recce unit the medical officer wears their khaki beret but with a bronze Royal Army Medical Corps badge on a backing of that corps' traditional dull cherry red.*

(Right) *NCO's sleeve insignia worn on Blouse, Battledress, Serge: yellow on green Reconnaissance Corps shoulder title, 43rd (Wessex) Infantry Division insignia, green/yellow arm of service strip, unofficial wireless operator's badge, and corporal's chevrons. Despite the massive military bureaucracy, large numbers of insignia, titles, flashes, and badges of trade, qualification or skill were adopted at unit level without official authority. (Given that, e.g., 1st Royal Dragoons managed to wear a wholly unauthorised grey beret for a matter of years in the Middle East and Italy, this is not surprising.)*

Officer's Camp Kit

(Right) *Autumn 1944: an officer on a brigade staff makes the best of temporary quarters somewhere in the Low Countries. On receipt of the King's Commission - and an allowance - the fledgeling Army officer had to purchase not only the required uniform items but also a range of specified "camp kit". His rank permitted the possession of collapsible camp furniture including bed, bedroll, sink and bath set, canvas bucket, chair, possibly a table, and suitable means to carry this impedimenta. Here a canvas and leather valise sits at the head of the camp bed, a tin trunk to the left among the kit bags; he uses a rolled sleeping bag as a pillow, and the bedroll itself as part of the bedding. His billet has been made a little more homely with additional touches acquired from the locals or found abandoned. Obviously, this kind of camp kit was not taken into the fighting lines by junior infantry officers, and in their case it spent much of its time packed away on the transport with the unit rear echelon.*

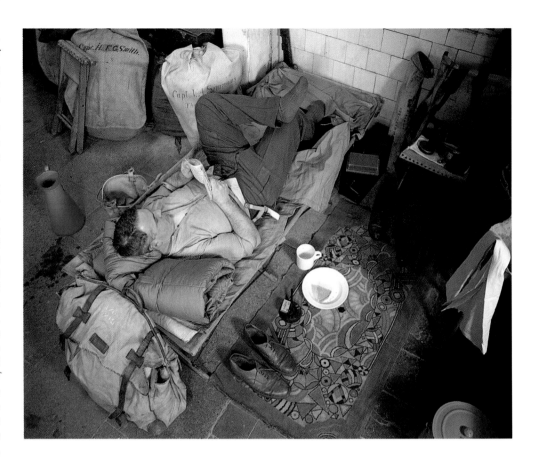

(Left) *Seated at his makeshift bureau, our officer attends to paperwork and correspondence. A rifle, property of the building's previous occupants, leans in the corner. Note the officer's pullover shirt, minus its detachable collar. The trousers show that his battledress has been made up in gabardine, the same fabric as service dress - a practice adopted for the sake of smartness and comfort by some more senior officers. His khaki elasticated braces are unusual in that they are produced for the Army QM Department for sale to officers.*

(Below) Detail of camp bed and bedroll both open and folded. The bedding is rolled around the dismantled bed and secured by long straps passing through loops on the outside of the roll. The bedroll itself could act as a bag with clothing and small items placed inside before it is rolled around the bed (and perhaps other camp furniture).

(Above) The folding sink and bath frame being used with the sink canvas; note the typical light wood, black metal fittings and light green fabric of camp furniture. When the bath was used the frame opened out further and the larger bath canvas was looped over it. Noteworthy is the quilted sleeping bag, at right, which fits inside the canvas bedroll for transit, along with two blankets and a camp pillow. This bag is Ordnance - marked, and was therefore procured from the Quartermaster, who sold a range of camp kit as an alternative to purchase from commercial outfitters. The quality and price of the items sold by civilian suppliers would vary to reflect the very different status, and resources, of a subaltern or a colonel; equipping officers with all their necessities was big business.

(Right) Personal items belonging to our staff officer's brigadier. A whole range of officers' uniform items appear to have been produced by the Quartermaster from 1944, including detached collar shirts like that hanging over the brigadier's BD blouse. Officers' shirts and ties were worn in a variety of khaki shades, styles and fabrics depending upon regimental custom or individual taste and wealth. This blouse has also been tailor - made, though in the standard serge fabric. Note brown ankle boots also made for the QM for officers or senior NCOs. Leaning to the left of the chair is a sink and bath unit still in its canvas carrying bag.

Officer's Service Dress, 1944

(Above) Rome, June 1944: the Italian capital was liberated on 4 June, being saved from destruction by the withdrawal of German forces. The delights offered by Rome were fully appreciated by the Allies, and the city soon became a major rest and recreation centre. Many Italians welcomed the Allies with open arms and were happy to change sides; here an Italian serving with the US forces as a noncombatant interpreter helps out two British officers enjoying the sights. For this first chance of civilised living in many months, perhaps years, the two 8th Army veterans have dusted off their service dress.

(Above right) Other than its closer cut and straight legged trousers the standard SD had changed little from that worn during the Great War. Countless minor regimental variations existed, from the cut away front of Scottish regiments to the distinctive button arrangements of Foot Guards; but most differed little from the uniform worn here by a captain of The Royal Fusiliers. Pleated breast pockets were closed with three - point flaps, while the capacious "bag" or "bellows" skirt pockets had no pleats and straight flaps; the sleeves were finished with a pointed decorative false cuff. Pocket and other buttons were all of regimental pattern; regi-

mental bronze collar badges were worn on the lapels, and a regimental badge on the SD cap. This captain's campaign ribbons are those of the 1939 - 43 Star, the Africa Star and the Italy Star.

(Right) This more recently arrived lieutenant of the Royal Army Service Corps wears the austerity pattern of service dress first introduced in March 1942. Similar in cut to the standard SD, it differed in having unpleated breast pockets, internal skirt pockets with buttonless flaps, and plain cuffs to the sleeves. A matching cloth waistbelt allowed wear without the necessity of the Sam Browne, an expensive accessory. Despite orders to the contrary tailors could often be persuaded to make up new uniforms in the pre - austerity style. This officer's headgear is the universal field service cap, often called a sidecap or forage cap. Identical in design to that worn by other ranks, it is made of the same fine barathea fabric as the tunic and has bronze buttons and cap badge.

(Opposite page)
The best way to see any beautiful city is undoubtedly in the company of a charming local guide....Officer's service dress worn as a walking - out uniform.

Rifle No 4

August 1944: a youthful rifleman from the 1st East Lancashires, 71 Brigade, 53rd (Welsh) Division takes part in house clearing. Volunteers could enlist at the age of 17½, and could be sent overseas a year later. British infantry casualties were extremely heavy, and replacements were soon arriving much less well prepared for combat than the long-trained units which first landed. (An officer with 4th Bn, KSLI, which suffered badly in late July, recalled that in early August his company received 40 replacements - and had three days to turn former coastal artillery gunners into combat infantry.)

His weapon is the No 4 rifle, a development of the SMLE which had been under trial since before the war but which did not begin widespread issue until after 1941; it was standard in the NW Europe campaign, but was late to arrive in quantity in Italy. Simpler to produce than the SMLE but essentially similar, its immediate external differences are the muzzle, the grooved upper forestock, and the aperture rear sight - here the simple flip-up battle sight version. Note (lower inset) the spike bayonet scabbard held into the old pattern webbing frog by a little leather strap, slotted at one end and with a pierced brass tab at the other, which fits over the scabbard stud. The old sword bayonet frog was not replaced; other methods of adapting it for the smaller scabbard were to cut a slot for the scabbard stud in the upper web loop of the frog; or to stitch down the loops to narrow the aperture for the scabbard.

The sleeve insignia (upper inset) of 4th Welch Regiment, 160 Brigade is interesting on two counts. It shows the 53rd Div. practice of printing the divisional insignia on the same khaki drill patch as one, two or three arm of service strips indicating the seniority of the brigade within the division; some 53rd patches also have one, two or three vertical bars below the brigade strips, to indicate battalion seniority within the brigade. The "little saucepan" flash beneath is a good example of an entirely unofficial but universally worn battalion insignia. Sospan Fach begins the chorus of the rousing Welsh language nonsense song which was the anthem of the battalion's local Llanelli rugby football supporters.

Light Respirator

(Right) Respirator, Anti - Gas, Light; the Mk I, introduced in 1942, saw limited service in North Africa. This Mk II version was issued in 1943 and was carried in action by many combat troops from D - Day onwards. The light respirator did away with the long tube and the large filter canister carried on the chest in a haversack, substituting a lighter, side - mounted canister. Being smaller, the screw - on canister's operational life was reduced; but it was easily replaced by a trained soldier, even during use in areas of gas contamination. The face mask was essentially that of the earlier box respirator.

(Below) Light respirator with the contents of its canvas case. Although with hindsight the gasmask was merely an encumbrance, the threat of chemical warfare had to be taken seriously. This was the time when Nazi propaganda was constantly threatening the Allies with "secret weapons", some of which were all too real. A man's respirator was considered an essential piece of equipment, and a second red identity disc was issued and tied to the muzzle of the facepiece. Note the blue/grey finish of the muzzle and canister. The case could be worn slung on its strap, and sometimes tied steady against the body with the cord provided; or slipped sideways onto the waistbelt by means of loops on the back of the case. Included in the case are a handful of cotton waste for applying Ointment Anti - Gas, and a pair of eyeshields; six of these were carried – sometimes three clear three tinted – in the card envelope tucked into a pocket inside the case. The round tin of anti – misting cloth for the eyepieces fitted into a pocket inside the bottom of the case. Tins contain eight tubes of No 2 and No 5 anti – gas ointment (issue of later numbers succeeded earlier types), two of which were carried in the outside pockets.

Officer's Webbing Equipment

(Below) Autumn 1944: a pause during the advance of the "Desert Rats". A captain of 1st Bn, The Rifle Brigade (which provided the Motor Battalion for 7th Armoured Division's 22nd Armoured Brigade) wears the Mk III helmet, and battledress of prewar pattern. However, the collar has been faced with serge and tailored permanently open - a private modification frequently seen. His embroidered rank pips are in black on Rifle green, as is his RIFLE BRIGADE shoulder title. Beneath the jerboa divisional insignia is the Rifles' green arm of service strip. The 1937 pattern web equipment was a universal set designed to meet the needs of all arms and all ranks. The officer's set was inspired by that sold during World War I by the Mills Equipment Company. It used the web waistbelt common to all sets, braces, brace attachments, binocular case, compass pouch, pistol ammunition pouch, holster, and officer's valise (a small pack with single buckle closure, originally converted from 08 pattern small packs). The set was generally finished off with a mapcase, the standard pattern being a board with clear plastic cover and webbing flap, later replaced by an all - web version. Our captain wears the basic set; the shoulder braces are of the late economy pattern with bakelite replacing the earlier brass tips.

It should be emphasised that in battle many officers modified their dress and equipment. One former NCO recalls the arrival of a new platoon commander in July 1944 after murderous fighting at Hill 112 in Normandy - his third lieutenant in five weeks, by which time only nine men of the platoon were left of the 36 who had landed. His lieutenant wore a pair of corduroy slacks, a thick woollen pullover with his rank pips prominently displayed, and a non - issue pistol buckled round his waist; his beret was the only regulation item.

(Right) The prescribed method of wear was with the holster and ammo pouch on the left and the binoculars and compass pouch on the right; in practice they were often reversed, as here, or combined in other ways according to personal preference. Compass and ammo pouches were outwardly similar, the former having a rigid frame and padded interior to protect the sensitive instrument. Later manufacture binocular cases had these side buckles which allowed the attachment of a brace for slinging it from neck or shoulder.

(Left) The only items unique to the officer's set were the valise, binocular case and compass pouch, although the latter two were occasionally issued to other ranks whose duties required them. This officer carries the valise and an early pattern binocular case. Typical of the relaxed approach to uniform accepted by some front line units, he wears an OR's issue pullover and has acquired Canadian issue BD trousers. The revolver is the .38 Enfield No 2 Mk I; having a hammer spur, this early weapon can be used single - or dou- ble - action. Neither method makes it a realistic battlefield weapon; many officers acquired Sten guns, and some substituted or added a basic pouch to their webbing.

(Below) Service binoculars. These came in several variants (some dating back to the Great War) which would fit into the webbing binocular case. Those that would not were generally issued with their own leather cases; these included the more powerful types issued to units such as the Royal Artillery.

Barathea BD & Economy Webbing

Winter 1944/45: a Grenadier Guards major from 21st Army Group HQ staff is visiting the front line. He recalls his days as a company officer well enough to borrow an OR's rifle and basic webbing set so as not to stand out in a sniper's sights - although the open collar and tie spoil the effect.

His battledress **(see inset above)** is privately tailored in fine barathea to the prewar pattern; he has had the epaulettes replaced on his promotion to major, so as not to show unsightly marks of his former three pips. Note also the economy pattern of web brace with folded and fully stitched junction of broad and narrow sections; earlier patterns had one - piece woven or two - piece pre-shaped stitched sections. A close look **(above left)** also reveals that the brass keeps each side of the waistbelt buckle have been replaced by web loops. These, and the later economy pattern belt with gunmetal alloy replacing the brass fittings, saw only limited issue in NW Europe.

(Inset left) Officer's Field Boot, with double buckle integral gaiter flap and apron - fronted uppers. An Ordnance pattern available for sale from RAOC officers' clothing shops, it was introduced in the mid - war period but was never particularly popular.

Hospital Dressing Gown & Pyjamas

Winter 1944/45: casualties - of wounds, or perhaps frostbite in the bitterest weather for years - recovering in a base hospital improvised in a recently liberated area, employing suitable buildings such as a warehouse. Hospital issue pyjamas in striped flannelette had buttoned jackets, and trousers with a drawstring waist. Details of stripe colour and type of button varied between manufacturers. For seriously disabled patients there was an alternative grey wool sleeved top termed the Smock, Helpless Patients, which laced at the back. A Hospital Dressing Gown was issued in hospital blue wool cloth; like the suit of hospital blues, it was probably intended to draw the attention of others to the fact that they were in the presence of a wounded soldier. Brown leather sheepskin lined slippers were also produced for hospitalised casualties.

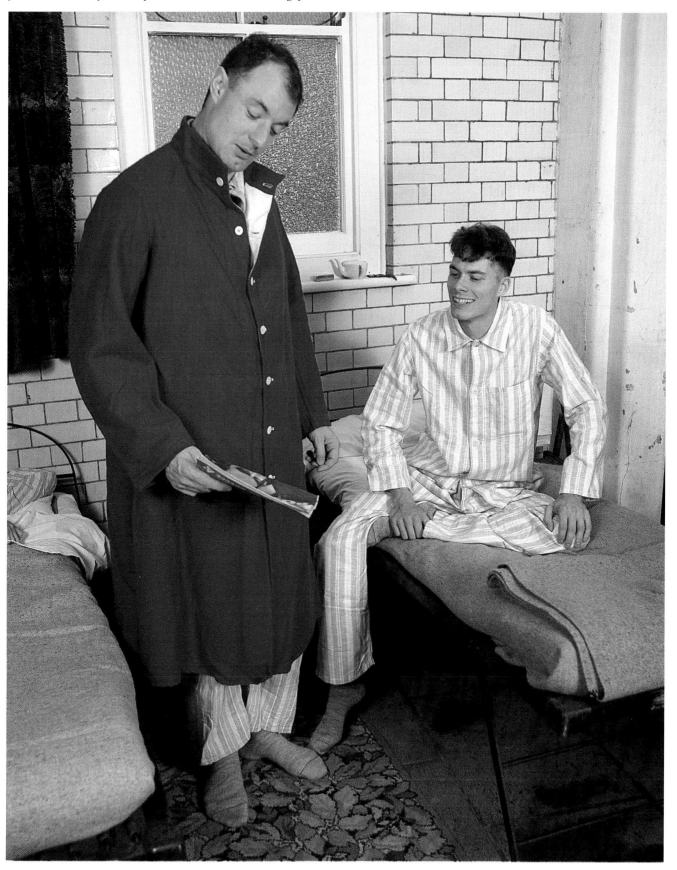

2 inch Mortar

Originally, in its prewar format, the 2in had most of the refinements (and disadvantages) of larger calibre mortars. However, it was soon simplified by reducing the size of the baseplate, deleting the collimating sight, and reducing the weight from 19lbs to 10½lbs, making it a perfectly practical weapon for the infantry platoon. The 2½lb bomb had a maximum range of 470 yards, and standard rate of accurate fire was eight rounds per minute. A shortened 14in barrel version was issued to Airborne troops, the shorter barrel reducing the range to 350 yards.

(Right) Moving into action, an infantry section advances under the cover of smoke laid by the 2in mortar team with the platoon headquarters section. The No 1 has aligned the mortar using the white line painted down the tube - accuracy will depend on his experienced eye. He is preparing to discharge the weapon using the firing lever; this was often made easier by the attachment of a short lanyard.

(Left) The standard 21in barrel version of the 2in mortar, showing its end cap and sling secured by the same carbine hook as used on the Bren gun. On the rounds different body colours, striping and nose caps identified various HE fillings, smoke, signal and illuminating bombs. This is a green - painted smoke round; HE were bronze-brown, signal rounds stone grey or black, and illuminating flares unpainted white metal. The bomb was projected by a ballistite cartridge inserted into the tail tube. (The padded mat illustrated here was supplied as part of the sleeping system, employed mainly by rear echelon troops as it was too bulky for infantry.)

(Right) Triple compressed card-board tubes with nailed tin strapping and wooden wedges, for carrying six 2in mortar rounds; this carrier was used throughout the war. The web strap passed completely round the edges of the carrier, providing a carrying handle at the top and fixing points for the tube end caps.

(Below) Section advance. The mortar and one ammo carrier were a reasonable load for one man, and his No 2 carried at least 12 rounds; but the section riflemen usually had to carry extra ammunition. Note here the later pattern six - round carrier introduced in the last winter of the war, with the tubes supported in a brown-painted metal frame.

Snow Camouflage

White clothing, the sole purpose of which was to help the soldier blend in with snow - covered terrain rather than providing any additional warmth, was first used by the British Army on the Western Front during World War I. During World War II the Army issued two basic types of snow camouflage (neither of which were available for the Norwegian campaign of 1940). A simple light-weight cotton two - piece suit lacked all external features and equally lacked any insulation value; this meant that it had to be worn over suitable warm clothing such as pullovers and BD, or the heavy-weight wool duffle coat - a short coat that was less practical than the smock due to its bulk and weight. The heavier set is distinguishable by the pockets on the smock and trousers, and provided a degree of insulation and windproofing.

(Right) The lightweight snow suit was of a very basic pattern, without pockets. The neck opening of the pullover smock was fastened with a single hook and eye; the simple hood was adjustable with a drawtape. Although the hood was sufficiently large to fit over the steel helmet a white helmet cover was also frequently worn. The trousers were also of a very simple design, pocketless and adjustable at the waist with a drawtape.

(Far right) If the large hood was worn over the steel helmet it tended to restrict head movement and lateral vision, a separate white helmet cover being better suited to combat use.

(Below) Smock, Camouflage, Snow: one of a series of similar garments which varied only in their colour, this windproof smock provided a degree of warmth as well as camouflage, and its four - pocket hooded design made it a functional item. Snow camouflage was generally worn for patrol work rather than extended operations; khaki web equipment would break up any camouflage by showing as distinct angular edges, and was therefore normally discarded in favour of carrying grenades and ammunition in smock pockets or bandoliers. Although slightly smaller than that of the lightweight smock the hood of this pattern could also be worn over the helmet, but its size made it even more restrictive.

(Below left) Cap, Comforter. A practical and popular item made of khaki wool, originally issued to all ranks of the Army but eventually restricted to field units and those whose duties required additional warm clothing. When pulled out to its full length it could be used as a short scarf or neck seal; when rolled up, its tubular construction made it a comfortable and versatile cap. (Photographs confirm that there was also some late issue to British troops of the US Army "beanie" wool cap.)

(Above right) The Jersey, Heavy Wool was issued as part of the cold climate clothing. Its excellent insulating properties meant that it was often used only by static personnel such as drivers and sentries. Troops engaged in active patrol work or skiing often found that the issue shirt and BD provided sufficient warmth, keeping the jersey for wear during rest stops when the body temperature would rapidly fall.

(Right) A Royal Artillery gunner from a 5.5in battery dons a Coat, Duffle. Intended for use only in the coldest of environments, this garment, although less restrictive than the old Tropal coat, still caused the wearer to overheat if it was worn during any strenuous activity. It was well suited to sedentary tasks or periods of inactivity.

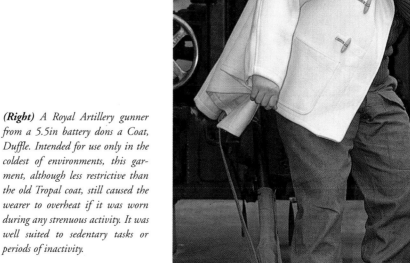

3 inch Mortar

(Right) Holland, winter 1944/45: a crew from the mortar platoon of the support company of an infantry battalion prepare for action. The soldier setting the dial sight holds the leather muzzle cover; at his feet is the leather case for the sight itself.

(Below) By 1944 the platoon's six 3in mortars are being taken into action in Universal carriers. The three sections of the weapon - barrel, baseplate and bipod - have been taken from the carrier and set up in a hollow offering some concealment. The 42lb baseplate was carefully placed on a firm footing and "bedded in" with a first ranging shot, so that once firing for effect has commenced there will be no shifting to throw the weapon off its intended trajectory. Ranging shots are bringing the mortar onto the target by a combination of map reference plotting and observation of the fall of shot, reported back to the platoon officer standing by the carrier - in this case over a No 38 radio set. In addition, a landline telephone is carried in each vehicle. A skilled team should be able to locate the target in five minutes.

The bombs themselves weigh 10lbs; they have two different strengths of propellant charge for use depending upon range. Operational ranges are from 500 to 2,750 yards, and when delivering rapid fire a tube can put up to 15 rounds per minute on to the target. Resupply of ammunition from support vehicles some distance away will be carried out with the help of any available riflemen commandeered for the task by the officer: the quantity of ammunition consumed is too great for the crew alone to handle.

(Right) Several cases of bombs have been made ready; the heavyweight cardboard triple tubes - identical in all but size to those used for 2in mortar ammunition - carry six bombs, and the yellow stripe identifies HE rounds. Note the discarded protective safety caps; these fit over the detonator in the nose of the bomb, and are unscrewed immediately before firing.

(Below) The No 38 radio set, also used in 1944/45 by some infantry and Airborne troops in place of the WS18. The radio fits into a distinctive webbing cradle with a shoulder sling; on top of the housing are the frequency tuner and inlet for the aerial. A second, smaller box takes the headset and throat mikes, which in turn connect to the battery box. This is carried in a web haversack similar to the 37 pattern small pack, which is slung at the operator's side when the radio is in use on the move. The effective range of the 38 set is about four miles.

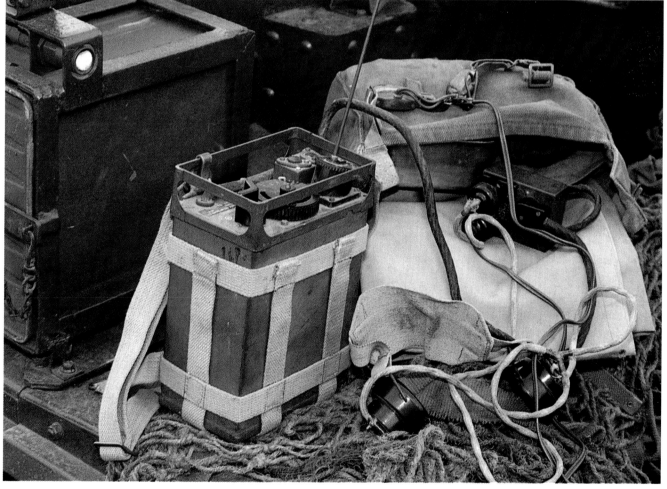

PIAT

January 1945: the last German offensive in the Ardennes has failed, and Montgomery's 21st Army Group gathers itself just inside Germany for a final thrust across the Rhine and into the heart of the Reich. Moving back into the line, an infantryman from a platoon headquarters section carries a PIAT - Projector Infantry Anti - Tank. This weapon, derived from prewar experiments, went into production at the end of 1942 and replaced the 5.5.in anti - tank rifle at platoon level. Unlike the US Army's "bazooka" rocket - launcher which performed the same task, the PIAT operated partly by mechanical force - a spring driving a metal rod or "spigot" which detonated a charge in the tail tube of a 3lb hollow charge bomb, throwing it 100 or 120 yards. Primarily an anti - tank weapon and capable in that role of knocking out the heaviest German tanks, it was also effective against blockhouses or any other defended buildings.

Cocking the PIAT before the first shot required the heavy spring to be pulled back; this was done by rotating the butt piece and pulling or pushing it away from the body of the weapon - usually by lying on the back with the feet braced on the butt, and compressing the spring using the strength of the legs and bowed body. The No 2 took

a bomb (from cardboard carrying tubes similar to those used for 3in mortar rounds), fused it, and placed it in the open forward trough, its tail tube fitting to grooves at the spigot aperture. Trigger pressure released the spring; the long rod flew forward with great force up the tail tube of the bomb, detonating the propellant charge, and keeping the bomb straight as it blew itself up the rod and out the front of the trough. The charge also drove the spigot back and recocked the spring. The PIAT had a fearsome recoil; cocking, getting close enough to a target to aim effectively, and controlled firing required considerable strength and nerve. Helmets were always worn, and heads tilted downwards to protect the face.

(Right) The No 1 carries both the PIAT and a Sten Mk II as his personal weapon.

(Below) Preparing to fire. The No 1 uses rudimentary rear aperture and front post sights, steadying the weapon on its detachable monopod and bracing it tightly with both hands; the No 2 is about to insert the bomb in the trough. The cork hanging below the trough was for insertion into the spigot aperture when the weapon was not in use.

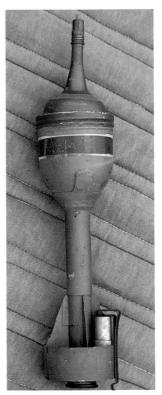

(Below) PIAT bomb: the painted red marking indicates a live round, the other coloured bands the type of explosive. Clipped to the fins for transit is a tube holding the detonating fuse, which is screwed into the nose immediately before use.

Utility Denims

By early 1945 the fortunes of war have brought this King's Own Scottish Borderers veteran a set of sergeant's stripes. In a battle - scarred house he takes the opportunity of a lull in the fighting to clean his weapon. He has taken the weighted, looped cord "pull - through" and an oil bottle from the butt trap of the rifle, and is using the cord to pull an oiled piece of "four by two" flannelette up the bore.

By the latter half of 1944 the utility pattern denim battledress uniform - like the serge counterpart alongside which it was designed in 1940 - was very common; it had first come into use in 1942. The utility denims differed very little from the previous pattern: breast pocket pleats had been deleted, the left thigh map pocket had an exposed button, and the trousers no longer had belt loops or tightening tabs at the bottom of the leg. The final modification to the trousers came in 1945 when the outer seams were left open behind the waist pockets to allow access to the pockets of the serge BD trousers if they were worn underneath.

While they were used extensively in action in NW Europe by corps troops such as engineers and artillery, it was unusual - though not unknown - for denims to be worn by infantry "up the sharp end". They were much more widely worn in combat in Italy during the summer months. Note the printed sergeant's stripes, part of a whole range of printed insignia worn by soldiers from 1943 onwards. Though the stripes are worn on both sleeves here, NCO rank was sometimes displayed on only one sleeve of fatigue clothing.

Camouflage Tank Crew Oversuit

Of an identical design to the tan version, the Oversuit, Tank Crews, Camouflage differed only in its camouflage finish. It was designed towards the end of the war for temperate climates, not for jungle operations - for which a lightweight jungle green suit was developed.

The two full - length zips from neck to ankle allowed it to be put on and taken off more easily; they also gave greater access to wounds when treating casualties. The close - up (note 1st King's Dragoon Guards cap badge on black RAC beret) shows these well; also the left breast pocket with pencil loops, and the overall appearance of the camouflage pattern, generally resembling that used for the windproof camouflage suit and the Denison smock.

Armoured Unit and Formation Insignia

(Above) Against the backdrop of a Churchill Mk IV infantry tank, a Royal Tank Regiment officer and trooper orientate a map to the local terrain. The Churchill was widely used by the independent Tank Brigades which operated in direct support of infantry units; it thus saw more continuous action than the tanks allocated to Armoured Brigades, which tended to operate at high intensity for relatively short periods at a time. The Churchill was much more heavily armoured, slower, and had better obstacle - crossing capability than the Sherman which became more or less standard in the Armoured Brigades in 1943 - 44. Apart from gun tanks it was produced in many variants including the Crocodile flamethrower, Ark bridgelayer and various support tanks such as the Armoured Vehicle Royal Engineers, Armoured Recovery Vehicle, and Beach Armoured Recovery Vehicle.

(Left) The insignia of a major of 44th Royal Tank Regiment, 4th Armoured Brigade. On his epaulette the major's rank crown on cavalry yellow backing is sewn over the yellow and red regimental flash of 44th RTR; the regiments of the RTR did not wear a shoulder title. The black on white jerboa insignia identifies the 4th Armoured Brigade; below this is the red and yellow arm of service strip of the Royal Armoured Corps as a whole. The white on khaki World War I tank badge was worn on the right sleeve only by all ranks and personnel of the Royal Tank Regiment. 4th Armoured Brigade - veterans of North Africa, Sicily and Italy - was a XII Corps asset which operated in support of but independently from the Armoured Divisions; it fought all the way from Normandy to the Elbe, and in 1944 - 45 comprised The Royal Scots Greys, 3rd/4th County of London Yeomanry (Sharp-shooters), and 44th RTR.

(**Right**) Trooper of 7th Royal Tank Regiment, 31st Tank Brigade. The red over green epaulette flash identified 7th RTR, and men of this unit also wore a black lanyard at the left shoulder. The "diabolo" shape was worn in various colours by several Tank Brigades, all in green by the 31st. The RAC arm of service strip was worn with yellow to the front on both sleeves. The RTR tank badge would also be worn on this man's right sleeve. 7th and 9th RTR of this brigade landed in Normandy on 21 June 1944; after heavy fighting in July and August both regiments were transferred to 34th Tank Brigade in early September, but 7th RTR later returned to 31st (now Armoured) Brigade as part of 79th Armoured Division, converting to Churchill Crocodile flamethrower tanks in January 1945.

(**Below**) Map box. This small case for maps was issued to tank crews, the contents varying depending on the theatre of operations. This case contains map coverage for France, Belgium and Holland in the 1:100,000 and 1:250,000 series.

Despatch Rider, 1945

(Right) It is spring 1945, and a motorcycle messenger from HQ London District awaits further instruction in the grounds of a country house loaned to the military as a headquarters for the duration of hostilities. Around his steel motorcyclist's helmet are his motor transport goggles with their distinctive teardrop shape. With his BD blouse of prewar pattern he wears Breeches, Motorcyclist made of heavy whipcord fabric with kid leather reinforcing patches on the inside of the legs. They were also made in cavalry twill or green twill fabric. Where they taper at the calf a khaki drill band with a vent is secured by two buttons (these were unfastened to give greater room when pulling the breeches over the feet). Positioned high on the right thigh is a button - fastened field dressing pocket. He is armed with a webbing pistol set.

(Below) Detail of the interior cradle of the steel Helmet, Motorcyclist.

(Bottom) Other ranks' GS cap with Royal Signals badge (the Mercury figure, known as the "Signals Jimmy") on a blue cloth backing for smartness. This particular cap is of late manufacture, being made from the same fabric as battledress. Earlier examples produced from 1943 were made in the same smoother fabric as the FS cap.

(Below) The insignia worn in the now usual configuration of corps or regimental shoulder title, formation or organisation patch (HQ London District), and arm of service strip.

The white on blue Royal Corps of Signals title was officially changed to ROYAL SIGNALS at the end of 1944, but such details took months to work through in practice.

Military Police

The spring of 1945 saw the 2nd Army fight their way across the Rhine and advance steadily across northern Germany as far as the Elbe. The Army headquarters advanced with the fighting units, occupying whatever buildings or enemy establishments became available.

In the field The Corps of Military Police were responsible for a wide range of tasks from security, discipline and traffic control to prisoner handling. This sergeant of the Provost Wing, identifiable by the distinctive red cover to his SD cap, has been assigned to providing security for a part of 2nd Army headquarters; here he is giving directions to a captain in the Rifle Brigade wearing a I Corps shoulder patch. Typical of the high standard of turn - out expected of MPs, his uniform consists of a well - pressed utility pattern BD blouse and trousers, "bulled" ammunition boots, and white-blancoed webbing with highly polished brasswork. He wears the black on red C.M.P. shoulder title above the patch of 2nd Army; just visible on his chest is the Africa Star ribbon with the silver numeral 8 testifying to his previous service with 8th Army; and a whistle chain emerges from his breast pocket.

The 9mm Mk II Sten is secured to the rear of the 37 pattern waistbelt by a pistol lanyard clipped to the handguard. This stopped the weapon being snatched from the MP, and also avoided the risk of the lanyard being used as a garotte - an obvious problem when worn around the neck.

(Right) *The red cover to the standard Service Dress cap was highly visible and left little doubt as to the wearer's role.*

(Below right) *This MP's web equipment serves no purpose other than to add to his martial appearance and general smartness. As no pouches or holster are worn, the brace attachment alone serves as a fixing point for the brace worn diagonally across the body. Meticulous attention has been paid to polishing and blancoing. (In addition to the visible surfaces, all reverse faces would also have been polished bright - and so, more than likely, would the underside of the boot instep.)*

(Below) *The brassard was worn on the right arm below any rank chevrons. The brassard and cap cover were duty items, being removed when not actually on provost duties.*

Variations in Officer's Service Dress

At the close of the war in Europe a group of officers congregate in a mess anteroom at the end of the evening, exchanging their experiences over a last relaxing drink. The officer to the right of the hearth wears service dress of a cut often worn by the cavalry, in this case the 5th Inniskilling Dragoon Guards. The tunic skirt pockets are concealed and the pocket flap is angled so that it slopes front to back. The breast pockets are not pleated, and have rounded point flaps more like those of a utility style tunic. On the cuffs there are two buttonholes and regimental buttons, and the usual pointed overlay of fabric is omitted.

The officer resting on the mantelpiece wears shoulder insignia on his service dress tunic, in this case the patch of 2nd Army; at that date this practice was more common than is generally believed. He is wearing a matching fabric belt with his tunic rather than the Sam Browne.

The seated lieutenant has returned to his parent regiment, The Royal Welch Fusiliers, of which the 10th Battalion was reformed as the 6th (Royal Welch) Parachute Battalion in 1942 (later, 6th Bn, The Parachute Regiment). He retains the parachute qualification brevet on his right sleeve. Fixed to the collar is the regimental distinction of the RWF, a "flash" of black silk ribbons.

(Right) Detail of Army pattern wings worn by qualified pilots; our major of the 5th Dragoon Guards has formerly served on flying duties, probably with the Glider Pilot Regiment of Airborne Forces. Note regimental buttons and collar badge of the 5th DG.

(Left) Close - up of Army parachute qualification brevet in white on khaki fabric; lieutenant's metal rank pips; Royal Welsh Fusiliers bronze collar badge; and the regiment's distinctive black ribbons. The origin of these can be traced to the early 19th century, when the Army abandoned the practice of wearing a "queue" or pigtail of greased and powdered hair; this had been bound in black silk to keep the powder off the collar of the red coat. The 23rd Foot (later RWF) were overseas for many years when the order to discontinue its use was announced; after their return they obtained the right for officers and some NCOs to continue to wear silk ribbons, a distinction extended to all ranks in 1900.

(Right) Guards officer's pattern service dress tunic, with flat patch skirt pockets and unpleated breast pockets. The configuration of the front buttons varies with the particular regiment of Foot Guards: single spacing for the Grenadier Guards, in pairs for the Coldstream Guards, in threes for the Scots Guards, in fours for the Irish Guards, and, as here, in a single group of five for the Welsh Guards. The flat bottom button does not count, as it is normally concealed under the Sam Browne or fabric belt. Though not visible here, a group of five small buttons are also worn on each cuff. Officers of the Foot Guards do not wear collar badges on khaki service dress; and rank pips are of special regimental pattern.

Staff Officer's Service Dress, 1945

(Left) Officers of the rank of colonel and above were distinguished as being of staff rank by the use of a coloured band on the stiff service dress cap and matching gorget patches, the colour varying with the officer's department or corps - in this case, the scarlet of a brigadier on the General Staff. Colonels and brigadiers wore the same pattern of gorget patch, with a button bearing the Royal cypher of the reigning monarch and a line of "gimp" embroidery. Both these ranks wore the cap badge illustrated, regardless of department or corps: the King's crown surmounted by a lion. The rank of brigadier is identified by the three rank stars surmounted by a crown, these badges being slightly smaller than those worn by line officers so as to accomodate them on the epaulette. The cut of the uniform was as per regulations, there being no particular distinctions for staff rank.

Shortly after VE - Day this officer's tunic shows a fine array of ribbons marking service through two World Wars: Order of the British Empire (Military), Military Cross, British War Medal (1914 - 18), Victory Medal (1918), General Service Medal, 1939 - 45 Star, Africa Star (8th Army), Italy Star, Defence Medal, War Medal (1939 - 45), Officer of Legion of Merit (USA). The brigadier chats with a captain from the Rifle Brigade, identifiable by his black rank stars and the black Sam Browne with white metal fittings as worn by all Rifle regiments.

Cap band and gorget patch colours: Scarlet, Staff, & Royal Army Ordnance Corps post - Oct.1941 (dark blue pre - Oct.1941); bright blue, Royal Engineers; dull cherry, Royal Army Medical Corps; maroon, Royal Army Veterinary Corps; emerald green, Army Dental Corps; purple, Army Chaplains Dept.; primrose, Army Pay Corps; Cambridge blue, Army Education Corps.

(Right) Here, at one of the numerous inter - Allied conferences immediately following Germany's unconditional surrender in 1945, a Canadian lieutenant - colonel of the Queen's York Rangers (1st American) Regiment converses with a British brigadier, right. The brigadier wears the shoulder patch of HQ Southern Command (UK) on his well - tailored American War Aid BD blouse. The waist fastening of this particular blouse (hidden here) uses an American enlisted man's belt buckle rather than the normal British fastening.

The lieutenant - colonel (who has closed his BD collar, other ranks' style) displays the CANADA title worn by all Canadian military units except those whose unit title included the name of their country. The colourful regimental title is typical of the Canadian style, which allowed designs unique to the regiment. The red diamond identifies I Canadian Corps, whose units served in Italy. He wears the ribbons of the Military Cross, British War Medal (1914 - 18), Victory Medal (1918), 1939 - 45 Star, Italy Star, France & Germany Star, Defence Medal, Canadian Volunteer Service Medal, Jubilee 1935 Medal, Coronation 1937 Medal, Volunteer Medal, and Efficiency Decoration.

The difference in the colour and fabric of the two BD blouses is quite evident; both were greener than British - made blouses and used finer materials.

Staff Officer's Battledress, 1945

(Right) Officers who had received the honour of appointment as aides-de-camp to the reigning monarch wore the Royal cypher, GR VI, on the epaulettes of service dress, battledress and khaki drill uniforms; note the relative position of the cypher and the rank badges. The scarlet gorget patches are the small pattern for wear with shirts and on the BD blouse. The brigadier, evidently a veteran of the South-East Asia campaigns, wears the ribbons of the following decorations and medals: Order of the British Empire (Military), Military Cross, India General Service Medal, British War Medal (1914-18), Victory Medal (1918) with oakleaf of Mentioned In Despatches, 1939-45 Star, Pacific Star with silver rose indicating that he also qualified for the Burma Star, Defence Medal, War Medal (1939-45) with MID.

Tailored Battledress and Ties

Well before the war in Europe came to an end British soldiers were rebelling against the drab and unattractive appearance of the issue BD uniform. Strictly for walking out, the soldier's best or "tiddly" blouse often had the collar pressed open to reveal a privately acquired collar and tie, its khaki drill facings sometimes scrubbed pale. This practice gradually developed after the arrival from 1942 of American troops, who wore a shirt with collar and tie with their enviably smart open - collar Class A uniform. In the 8th Army in Italy, where US Army collar attached shirts were supplied to British troops in large numbers, their use with ties was condoned both on and off duty. Initially this practice was frowned upon, but by mid - 1944 the Army relented and produced a shirt with attached collar and a tie for walking - out dress. (The British version was inferior in style and quality to the American equivalents, which remained popular with Tommy.)

By 1945 battledress blouse collars were sometimes tailored permanently open, the interior being faced with serge to produce a distinctly officer -
like appearance. Tucks were tailored into the area above the breast pockets to improve the fit. The most fashion - conscious would have extra gussets tailored into the bottom of the leg seams to give their battledress trousers the slightly flared outline then popular "in civvy street". There was elaborate pressing of the tucks rising from the rear of the blouse waistband, and extra horizontal creases might be ironed across the back at shoulder level. By 1945 what the Army had introduced as a functional combat uniform had been adapted to suit current ideas of smartness by the subtle pressure of what was, after all, an army largely made up conscripted civilians - and civilians of a society which has always been tolerant of non-conformity. The whole progress of uniform between 1939 and 1945 reflects the pursuit of individuality out of uniformity.

(Right) A wartime wedding was the ideal opportunity to display non - regulation uniform refinements, and for the ladies to do their best with the available utility clothing or borrowed wardrobes.

(Below) The groom, at right, wears austerity BD with tailored collar and added facings. His sleeves display the title of The Suffolk Regiment in regulation infantry white on red, touched up with blanco; the 3rd Division patch means that he serves with the Suffolks' 1st Battalion in 8 Infantry Brigade. Below the infantry arm of service strip is the Suffolks' red and yellow Minden flash, celebrating the regiment's part in that battle on 1 August 1759; members of the regiment traditionally wore red and yellow roses behind the cap badge on the anniversary.

The best man, at left, has acquired a set of Canadian BD with its distinctive green hue. As a member of a mechanised infantry unit - 2nd Battalion, King's Royal Rifle Corps - he wears the khaki beret instead of the sloppy - looking GS cap worn by the groom; his Rifle - black cap badge is pinned through the KRRC's red backing patch. The regimental shoulder title, KRRC in red on dark green, surmounts the 4th Armoured Brigade patch and the Rifle green arm of service strip (the brigade insignia was worn by units not assigned to a division).

(Left & below) Wartime restrictions often made wedding receptions quiet affairs; alcohol was hard to find in any quantity, and at a time when the egg ration was one per person per week the "cake" might be a decorated wood or cardboard mock - up hired for the day.... Many settled for just a few drinks in the couple's new home. The groom is wearing the issue collar - attached shirt; it has no pockets and is of pullover type with a half - length buttoned placket; the issue tie is made of lightweight green cotton. The shoes are non - regulation, but were popular with those who could obtain them. The austerity pattern BD blouse has had the collar tailored open, the inner cotton lining being refaced with khaki serge. Additional fabric let into the lower legs is also evident. Such alterations could be classed as damaging or defacing War Department property, with subsequent disciplinary action and deduction of the cost of the items from a soldier's pay.

Demob Suit

A farewell to arms, 1945 - "So long, chum, and good luck". Shortly after the close of hostilities a prewar Regular is demobilised from the Army. He is classified category A for release, having served for the longest period, and so is amongst the first to return to civvy street. On arrival at a demobilisation centre - either a particular military establishment set aside for the task, or a suitable facility such as the exhibition hall at Olympia in London - the soldier is processed. His kit is handed in, and in exchange a grateful nation presents him with a suit of clothes tailored to Savile Row standards. "Demob" clothing was produced for the War Department and came with service -

type size labels or marked with the Ordnance arrow. Suits were made in the respective chest and waist measurements and either small, regular or large fittings. As immediate reference for the fitter suit sizes were given on an identifying label tacked onto the lower left sleeve of the jacket, which was removed once the suit had been accepted as fitting. The serviceman selecting his demob suit had a limited choice as to colour or style: a double - breasted three piece suit or a single - breasted jacket with flannels. He was also given a shirt with two matching collars and studs, a tie, shoes, a hat (either felt or a flat cap), and a raincoat. Raincoats had their own descriptive and size labels as for

suits. Hats and ties had tickets with the Ordnance mark and the date. For extra reference jackets, waistcoats and trousers had small internal paper sizing labels, e.g. 40 Reg and an identifying code number.

Thus refurbished, he leaves the barrack gate for the last time. In his pocket are his release book, a railway warrant, and his pay made up to date on completion of his military service.

A pal has come to see him off; note the GS cap with distinctions unique to 1st Battalion, The Duke of Cornwall's Light Infantry - scarlet cloth infill to the pierced silver badge, a large green badge backing, and green facing on the cap band.